About the Author

Giles Chance is the author of *China and the Credit Crisis: the emergence of a new world order* (2010) and *Doing Business in China* (Fifth Edition, 2022). Educated at Eton College, St Andrews University and Dartmouth College, New Hampshire, he served in the military, worked in the City of London as a banker, then with refugees in Somalia and Sudan, before becoming interested in China in the late 1980s. He has been an adjunct professor at Peking University and Dartmouth College.

Although the author and publisher have made every effort to ensure that the information in this book was correct at press time, the author and publisher do not assume and hereby disclaim any liability to any party for any loss, damage, or disruption caused by errors or omissions, whether such errors or omissions result from negligence, accident, or any other cause.

Living With Dragons
A Memoir of the Middle Kingdom

Giles Chance

Living With Dragons
A Memoir of the Middle Kingdom

Vanguard Press

VANGUARD PAPERBACK

© Copyright 2024
Giles Chance

The right of Giles Chance to be identified as author of
this work has been asserted by him in accordance with the
Copyright, Designs and Patents Act 1988.

All Rights Reserved

No reproduction, copy or transmission of this publication
may be made without written permission.
No paragraph of this publication may be reproduced,
copied or transmitted save with the written permission of the
publisher, or in accordance with the provisions
of the Copyright Act 1956 (as amended).

Any person who commits any unauthorised act in relation to
this publication may be liable to criminal
prosecution and civil claims for damages.

A CIP catalogue record for this title is
available from the British Library.

ISBN 978 1 83794 185 8

*Vanguard Press is an imprint of
Pegasus Elliot Mackenzie Publishers Ltd.*
www.pegasuspublishers.com

First Published in 2024

**Vanguard Press
Sheraton House Castle Park
Cambridge England**

Printed & Bound in Great Britain

To my family.

'Experience is a good school.
But the fees are high'

Heinrich Heine

FOREWORD

This book is about my twenty-year relationship with China between 1988 and 2008, which brought me failure, success, bitter disappointment, frustration, fascination, enlightenment, understanding and love. It made me a different person, probably a better one.

However, this book is not just about my engagement with China at a pivotal moment in its history. It's about taking your destiny into your own hands, trusting your judgement, and leaping into the unknown as an entrepreneur. It's about the intuition, the risk-taking, the leg work, and the luck that go hand in hand to make a business successful, and falling over and getting up. And it's about how family fits into the busy life of an entrepreneur.

I believe the lessons I learned in China, as it was beginning to re-emerge into the global economy, are examples for anyone doing business anywhere. The most important business lesson from China is what the Chinese call 'guanxi', and what the West calls 'networking'. Nothing important can be done in China without the right relationships. That's a good thought to take with you everywhere you go. Another lesson to take from the

Chinese is punctuality. In the thousands of private and business meetings I have had with Chinese people, I can hardly remember one occasion of tardiness on the Chinese side. To ensure punctuality — not too early, nor too late — means that Chinese people must inevitably wait sometimes for a few minutes before a meeting. That's impressive, because arriving on time is the ultimate in good manners. It implies that the other person's time is valuable, and it's a great way to get any meeting, business or private, off to a good start.

My journey began in 1984, in Washington, DC. I had been invited to a drinks party in a smart residential district by a Malaysian girl studying economics at Oxford and interning at the World Bank, as was I. I think her plan was that we would have supper together after the party and get to know each other better. But I spoilt her plan (I found out later) by going to the basement to find a beer. There, I met a Chinese girl. Born in Shanghai, she had grown up in Beijing, and had arrived in the United States in 1980 as one of the first people to emigrate from China soon after Mao died. She was studying for a doctorate in economics in New York. Like me, she was spending her summer at the World Bank. And she was beautiful.

In an earlier life, in the late seventies — towards the end of China's Cultural Revolution — I had been based in Hong Kong as a soldier. I had spent many days and nights on the Chinese border, looking over at the farms on the other side, and listening to the shouted harangues, interspersed with martial music and Chinese folksongs broadcast several times daily in each border village. I had seen exhausted, soaked Chinese 'illegal immigrants' who had been captured on Hong Kong's border hills, handed back to the Chinese Army each day at noon across a bridge which spanned the river running between British colonial Hong Kong and Mao's China. I often wondered what it was like over there.

But it was not until that muggy June evening, in Washington, DC, that I had met anyone from red China. The basement of the professor's house was large enough to contain a ping-pong table. I challenged her to a game, and she won, easily. The next day we had lunch together in the bank canteen and she won again, by capturing my heart. Ying and I were married three years and nine months later.

We visited China for our honeymoon at a time when Chinese trains still travelled at a maximum of forty miles per hour, Chinese bicycles still outnumbered cars by ten million to one, and everyone in China thought Westerners must be rich. First we stayed with my wife's parents in Beijing, then travelled by train around eastern China, stopping for a night or two in Wuxi, Shanghai, Suzhou and Hangzhou. I talked to many Chinese people through a hired interpreter because Ying, who wanted to enjoy herself and relax, abandoned the interpreter role after one day. My first reaction was that this weird civilization, with its strange, unfamiliar language, disgusting smells and delicious food (and it must be said, rather primitive accommodation) was so completely different to my own,

6,000 miles away, that when the time came to go back home, I would remember it as exotic and interesting, but not of particular importance.

Then, bit by bit, I realised that beneath the surface there was something significant going on. Among the tales of sadness, disappointment, waste and frustration I heard from the people I met, there was something else: an unstated but palpable determination not to slip back or stagnate, but to do better. To stand up, to make progress, to fulfil a destiny. Often faces bore a distinct expression: hopeful, yes, but also confident. There was a striking belief in China, and its potential: 'We're a big country, and if we want to, we can do anything. No one can stop us.'

Our trip was oriented around meeting Ying's family — parents, cousins, aunts and uncles — in Beijing, Shanghai and Wuxi, a town near Shanghai. In nearby Suzhou — a picturesque waterway town at one end of the Grand Canal which from 600 AD until it fell into disrepair in the 1850s, gave the northern based Chinese emperor access to the south, and which took rice, silk and concubines from the Yangtse basin to Beijing — we stayed in the government sanctioned guest-house, a palace of sorts, reserved for official guests. The food was great and the bed comfortable. And it was clean. In the 1930s it had been the residence of Yao Yicheng, one of Chiang Kai-Shek's mistresses before his Wellesley College educated wife, Mayling Soong, had persuaded him to become monogamous and Christian.

Our trip included Hangzhou; since the southern Song dynasty in the twelfth century Chinese poets had described it as 'Heaven on Earth', it was a place we thought we should see on our honeymoon. We stayed in the appropriately named and newly built Shangri-la hotel by the lakeside. It was while sightseeing on the west lake that I started to understand that China might have the will and energy to fulfil its destiny, even at a time when the average wage was less than a dollar a day.

Someone suggested that we visit the tourist office in Hangzhou. We did, and were then graced by a visit from the director of the tourist bureau. He was a tall man, about forty, intelligent, with an attractive smile. I liked him, and when he suggested taking us out in a boat on the lake we accepted immediately. As he took the oars and rowed us slowly out to a restaurant on an island in the centre of the lake, he explained that his city had big plans. A business park would be built in Hangzhou, with special tax advantages for rich foreigners (which he imagined me to be): no tax for three years, with tax breaks thereafter. The local government would help me find staff and would introduce me to customers. He made it sound easy.

Then we reached the island. We were told that it was where the former Cambodian King Sihanouk had lived for a short time, after he was ousted from his throne in 1970 by a US backed coup. Two young, pretty Chinese girls in dress traditional to the region met us and showed us to a table. Lunch, a beer or two, and the beautiful landscape — a lake, surrounded by hills, no droning traffic, buzzing aeroplanes or urban sprawl — made things look even better.

By the time we had been rowed back to the shore, I was intrigued. The director had done his job well. I spent the rest of the trip fantasising. What if China was on the way up? Just think what that would mean.

On the 24-hour train ride from Shanghai back to Beijing, a Taiwanese businessman shared our compartment. He was a luggage manufacturer who had moved his factory from Taipei to mainland China. His new factory was near the Chinese border with Hong Kong — near the fields I had been gazing at as a British soldier in Hong Kong more than a decade earlier. Business was very good, he said. Costs were a fraction of those in Taipei, and the erstwhile Chinese farmers, now factory workers, were grateful to earn real money, and knew how to work hard. He had begun expanding his business in China, and now was doing better than he had in Taiwan.

Back in Beijing, we prepared for our flight on Aeroflot to London, changing planes in Moscow. In 1988 no western airlines flew direct to Beijing, so on our way back we were expecting to spend several hours sitting in the Russian capital while we changed planes. We said goodbye to my in-laws in their small ground-floor flat inside the People's University in Beijing. My father-in-law, who was a professor of history (the leading expert on Chinese journalism since the 1840s, when foreign newspapers had entered China through the treaty ports) arranged a taxi for us. It was the university's only car, a

Red Flag saloon, made by No 1 Auto Company in northern China on a 1950s Russian production line, the engine supplied by Mercedes Benz. It was the best car you could find in China at that time that did not belong to a foreign diplomat.

At the airport we checked in our suitcases, and my wife followed me to the immigration channel. Between us, we carried three vases we had bought in Beijing, which we were reluctant to entrust to Chinese and Russian baggage handlers. I was the first to pass through the border control. Though the Chinese officials stared suspiciously at my British passport, they finally stamped it and waved me on. But when I turned around, I saw my wife arguing with another official. I quickly retraced my steps. She shouted across the barrier that her passport was out of order and her visa did not permit her to return to Britain. She would have to stay behind in Beijing, and go through whatever the procedures were to permit her to leave the country.

Should I stay with her? I thought quickly. Or should I get on the plane in the hope that she'll join me in a few hours, or days? I had been away for nearly a month from my job as an investment fund manager in London. I had used up all my annual leave. A trusted colleague had been buying, selling and holding while I was away, but I had started to worry about the markets. Would the colleague be doing the right thing? What was happening to the dollar? If I stayed in Beijing with Ying, it could be another month or even three before we were able to leave. (Remember: this was before the Internet).

I felt I had to get back to London, and trusted that Ying could fix everything in my absence. If not, I might have to say goodbye to my budding career in the City of London. I was thirty-six-years old. This train of thought passed through my mind in a couple of seconds. I told Ying. My new wife and I said goodbye to each other through the barrier, and I boarded the plane clutching all three vases.

It was a long flight, with a stopover in Moscow that seemed to last several days but was in fact only three hours. I had plenty of time to reflect. The Aeroflot Tupolev, twin engines at the back like the old Douglas DC-10, flew surprisingly well. The plane was full of Russian businessmen and tourists. The vases were not small, and the Russian crew allowed me to take far more than my fair share of cabin space, a kindness that compensated a little for the concern I was feeling at leaving my new wife behind.

The shock of our abrupt parting brought my warm feelings about China into sharp focus, and made me think more carefully. In London, as a fund manager responsible for many million dollars' worth of other people's money, I was paid to evaluate risks, and sometimes accept them. The incident that had just occurred at Beijing airport seemed a good example of the kind of unforeseeable risk I had been trained to avoid. My thoughts turned to making my own way — opening up my own business, perhaps in China. What would I be taking on? How much unpredictability could I expect?

During the impression-filled trip, I had spent several days with Ying's parents in their Beijing apartment. In Shanghai we had stayed in a hotel, not in someone's home. But we had spent time with the Shanghainese side of her family. We had also engaged in several lengthy conversations with people we had met in our guesthouses and hotels, and on the train journeys between Shanghai, Hangzhou, Wuxi and Beijing.

From these multiple encounters I developed a sense of the pattern of Chinese life, which appeared to revolve around families, small local communities and individuals. I guessed these tight relationship networks were the foundation of doing business in China, once the ground rules had been understood and obeyed, and once relationships had been established. But how would Chinese attitudes to foreigners, to their society and to each other react to the economic and social development I anticipated? Would China's evolution from an inward-looking, poor, centrally planned, occasionally violent society fundamentally alter the domestic rhythm of Chinese life I had observed?

Perhaps the anonymity of airports makes them good places for reflection. In Moscow I, an Englishman listening to not-understood announcements in Russian and observing the drab impersonality of his surroundings, couldn't have been more anonymous. I arrived from Beijing feeling lonely, full of doubt and confusion. A few hours later, I left for London with sprouting seeds of conviction. Clearly, there were risks in China. Were there not risks everywhere? Yet I felt there was something predictable about Chinese society that I warmed to: the durability of personal relationships, the unseen glue of ancient beliefs and customs, and the kind of solidarity formed by communities that have survived unimaginably tragic hardships. Also, I had the good fortune to be married to a Chinese woman, who I was sure would be a willing guide through the labyrinth of her country's customs and perceptions. By the time I reached London, I had decided I could live with the Chinese unknown and unknowable.

Looking back thirty years later, I think I was largely correct in believing that China's society would not fundamentally change as the country developed, and that the important ground-rules for social acceptance and progress would remain in place. Many older Chinese today lament the fact that the younger Chinese generation, the so-called millennials, have different values to their parents and grandparents, perceiving themselves to be independent, and that overseas travel and entertainment have more importance for them than thrift and hard work. Yet China remains a family-centred culture, in which the dual influences of Confucianism and Daoism, with their overtones of social conformity, obedience, family ties, respect for elders and inclination for balance and compromise still affect behaviour as profoundly as they ever did.

Today I see Chinese society like an onion, with the changes of the last forty years forming a new layer that covers the many others created by the multitude of Chinese experiences over the last several thousand years. Deep inside, the essence is unchanged. My first introduction to China, in the form of a whistle-stop tour with my wife by train around the country's eastern coastline, brought home the essential point about Chinese society, namely the importance of personal relationships.

Thirty years ago, the Chinese needed every kind of material assistance to modernise. Yet few western commercial enterprises and political institutions saw China as a good long-term bet, in which they should invest time and money. Westerners like me who placed their knowledge, international connections and resources at the disposal of the emerging China in those early days gained a privileged position, because the Chinese rewarded our faith in their future with their trust. By sharing a small part of China's historic, volatile trajectory from international pariah to global superpower, often when success seemed far away, I gained insights into China's hopes and fears. It's that story, and those insights, which I want to share in this book.

I

TAKING THE PLUNGE

Until 2020 I taught a class on doing business in China at America's Dartmouth College. I used to begin the first class by showing a few current slides of China. They included a chart of China's share of the profits of the six largest global car companies (between 20 and 45 per cent, depending on the company), pictures of the island archipelagos in the South China Sea occupied by China, and contested by the peripheral east Asian countries Japan, Vietnam, the Philippines, Malaysia and Brunei, and a graph showing the relative size of China's economy against those of the United States, Japan and the European Union, with China's clearly the world's largest, once local costs had been factored in. Then I asked the MBA students in front of me whether they saw China as an opportunity or a threat. Up until 2019, they almost all voted for 'opportunity'. But as China's economic and geopolitical power has grown, and after the COVID epidemic, the consensus has shifted from 'opportunity' to 'threat'.

When I first went to China thirty years ago, it was unimaginable how impressive its current position would be. The evidence of a country and a society shattered by conflict and battered by ideology was everywhere. First, the poverty and lack of infrastructure. The pungent stink of malfunctioning drains was ubiquitous. In 1999 my daughter, only aged five, refused to use the ladies' restroom in Beijing's Summer Palace, which consisted of an insanitary hole in the floor, even though it meant waiting until we got home an hour later. Everyone wore blue working overalls as if they were uniforms. No one had a telephone, and many families (the lucky ones) shared one bicycle. Many people still died of starvation. A Chinese university professor who grew up in a village in central China in the 1960s and 1970s told me recently that, as a child, he was always hungry. His diet year-in, year-out was rice, with a few vegetables and an egg once a week. He ate meat only at the New Year festival. The first time in his life that he ate fruit was when he went to Fudan University in Shanghai, aged nineteen.

Then, the enormous waste of human capital, locked into huge industrialised systems that produced little of marketable quality. Visiting a Chinese state-owned factory in 1991 reminded me of the soldiers' chant: 'We're here because we're here because we're here.' In 1994 I was shown a state-owned factory in central China by a successful local businessman who had executed a joint venture with a British company which made him a market leader, at least for the time being. The local government wanted him to amalgamate the failing state factory into his own enterprise, to maintain employment and tax revenue. On the tour, everyone seemed too busy to look at us. Clearly all the workers had been told to look active for our benefit. As I watched men in their forties and fifties pretending to operate machines with an obvious unfamiliarity, I could not help but smile at how surreal it seemed.

This — broken, inefficient, depressing — was the China I saw on my first visit in 1988. But from my previous experience I recalled something else, which I had thought at the time was significant. A few years earlier, as field director for Save the Children Fund in Sudan, Africa, I had become part of a basketball team. It was led by American aid workers and composed of foreigners like me, topped up with a couple of our Sudanese and Ethiopian employees. A few miles away from our base at Gedaref in eastern Sudan, on the border with Ethiopia, was a camp containing about two hundred Chinese. They had been sent to Sudan as part of Mao's campaign to place China at the head of what he called 'The Third World'. Their task was to build a road between the Sudanese capital Khartoum, and Port Sudan on the Red Sea, five hundred miles to the north-east.

We arranged to play basketball against the Chinese road workers. The game took place inside their camp, on a court they had made. The height difference in our favour made the game one-sided, but we were struck by their keenness, even though the odds were heavily against them.

We were seriously impressed by the excellent meal we sat down to afterwards, because our own meagre diet reminded us daily of the difficulty of obtaining a variety of fresh food. After supper they showed us their garden, containing a large quantity and variety of vegetables irrigated by water diverted from their ablutions, and fertilised by the waste from their latrines. Nearby we saw their goats, chickens and sheep. Their farm, for such it was, operated on a scale and complexity that outstripped anything else we had seen around Gedaref.

This display of enterprise and teamwork in the hot, waterless desert gave me an idea of what the Chinese were capable of. This was the picture I had in my mind's eye when I started to imagine later how introducing modern technology and capital into the Chinese system could work. It was an inspiration for what followed.

***

After the summer in Washington, DC when I had met my wife, I returned to Hanover, New Hampshire to complete my MBA. I had been fortunate enough to receive a Fulbright scholarship — a happy circumstance that made the two-year programme affordable — but it carried a downside. A condition of accepting the award was that I was obliged to turn down several tempting Stateside offers, and return to my home country, the United Kingdom, for a minimum two years after graduation.

In London I started work as an investment manager at a government owned organisation that looked after the financial assets of central banks and sovereign wealth funds around the world. I was well paid, and the job was interesting. But something was missing. My work a few years earlier with refugees in Africa had taken me out of the comfortable and privileged surroundings of my early years. When I began working with refugees in Somalia, then in Sudan, I entered a different, multi-cultural world, of hardship and extraordinary resilience, set in a landscape of harsh, simple beauty. Sudan was extremely poor before it found oil in the mid-1980s. Its refugees had strategic importance because they brought hundreds of millions of aid-dollars into the country. The head of the Sudanese Refugee Commission was therefore an important appointment, held by a senior and delightful Sudanese diplomat whom I came to know well. During one of our conversations, he told me that I would remember my time in his country as a special experience. He was right, and it changed me. I found it difficult to settle back into my old life in London. I was looking for another adventure.

Back home in the UK I put the vases away and went to my work, to find that my job had changed. In my absence, the office had been restructured, in response to the first-time regulation of the British investment management industry. I had ceased being the fund manager with responsibility for the Caribbean countries from the Bahamas to Aruba (good travel, great people), and now found myself as the new, first head of marketing, complete with assistants, office and bigger salary. It is a good indicator of the state of the investment management industry in those far-off days of the late 1980s that many investment managers hardly thought that marketing was necessary or important.

But by then I had begun actively imagining how I could start doing business with China. I sensed that something very big was starting there, that one-fifth of the world's population was starting to get its act together. What was it Napoleon had said, about China waking and the world trembling?

I thrashed around a few ideas, but then realised something a lot of people, including large multinationals, failed to grasp until they had been worn down to a shred, and had a lot of money taken away from them. I was thinking: 'Do something the Chinese need, but which they could not do themselves.' The Chinese are the world's greatest businesspeople. They combine relentless determination with great shrewdness and around-the-clock hard work. And at the point when I was embarking on my career with them, they were hungry, both literally and figuratively. Post-Mao and the great leap forward (or backward, as it were) they were keen to catch up to the rest of the developing world, their shackles off. Add to this their appetite for risk: they are also the world's keenest gamblers, with a willingness to fall flat on their face, get up and start again. As the Chinese say: 'Defeat is not bitter if you don't swallow it.'

***

Special Economic Zones (SEZ) are compact geographical areas located near China's borders, where low tax rates, simplified administrative procedures and zero tariffs on imported components encourage innovation and production for export. The first SEZ was set up in 1979 in Guangzhou (Canton), and was quickly followed by several others nearby, of which Shenzhen, just over the border from Hong Kong, has become the most successful. Many of these zones, which stretch from north to south down China's coastline, have attracted both foreign and Chinese traders and entrepreneurs, and have become wealthy as a result. They played a vital part in sparking China's economic growth in the 1980s and in driving the huge Chinese export boom that began in earnest in the late 1990s. Chinese exports grew by six times between 1998 and 2008, overtaking America's and making China the world's largest exporter.

I guessed that in their own house the Chinese were masters, but outside, in a foreign environment that deprived them of Chinese cultural assumptions and networks, they would be inclined to become weak and blind. China needed foreigners, to invest in China, to bring modern technology and business knowhow, to buy their products, and finally to provide the economic space for one-fifth of the world's population to grow into. It seemed to me that I could form a business that helped the Chinese deal with foreign companies, and helped foreigners deal with the Chinese. A kind of cultural-exchange agent, but with a commercial angle.

***

Ying, who had been stuck in China after our honeymoon for four weeks due to her exit visa issues, finally arrived home. It was wonderful to be reunited. In the pre-mobile-phone, pre-Internet era, and depending for communication on a single telephone on the university campus in Beijing where Ying was living with her parents, I had grown increasingly worried. We talked for hours over the long weekend, and I began to explain to her my plans for the future, hoping she would be as keen.

Every day I went to work thinking about it.

Meanwhile, Ying had had begun working as an economist for the treasury department of a large bank in London. Her doctoral thesis had been in foreign exchange, so her job consisted of analysing trends in dollar-sterling, dollar-deutschemark, dollar-everything. A large part of the bank's profits came from trading currencies, and her department had plenty of money to spend. But then, one day, the expensive economic data set she had bought off-the-shelf, with the bank's money, disappeared. Someone had deleted it from the department computer. She thought she knew who it was, but her boss did not back her up and extended her period of probation. She was furious, and resigned.

Ying had a doctorate in economics, but she had another more important qualification: a doctorate in survival. She had been one of the 50 children aged six selected to train for the Chinese gymnastic team in a special building in the centre of Beijing. Four years later, she was still there, long after most of the other children had quit the course or had been sent home. The tough gymnast training at such a young age gave her tremendous self-confidence and endurance.

She was eleven years old when the Cultural Revolution started in China. Her special athletic school closed, as did all the other Chinese schools and universities, and the nation entered into a crazy nightmare of struggle. After a period as a Red Guard, and wandering the streets of Beijing, Ying went to join her father, a professor, who had been sent away to the countryside as part of Mao's re-education programme. She spent two years living in a village in one of China's poorest provinces, Jiangxi, with hundreds of other emigrants from Beijing. At four a.m., they rose, and walked twenty miles to till the fields, often carrying nightsoil with them (one bucket between two people, suspended from a horizontal pole), which they would spread on the rice paddies. Work ended at three p.m., and after the twenty-mile walk back, they would eat rice with the local speciality — chillies.

After two years of this harsh environment, she returned to Beijing and was placed in another camp outside the city. There, she met someone who recognised her ability to write beautiful Chinese characters and quote

Chinese verse, skills taught to her by her intellectual father at an early age. This senior connection enabled her to leave the camp, and join the Arts and Crafts Bureau of the Beijing Government. There, she wrote speeches which were delivered, sometimes by her, to large groups of Chinese workers, extolling the virtues of Mao's regime and Chinese Marxism. In 1976, Mao died, the Gang of Four were arrested, and the Cultural Revolution ended. Ying's work changed. She started attending classes at Peking University (where her father was on the faculty) once the school reopened, and then spent two years studying Marxist economics at the Beijing College of Economics.

From there, she found her way to New York in 1980, via Hong Kong. With the help of her father's elder sister and her American husband, a head-hunter in New York City, she started studying accounting and then was accepted to study economics at university level. Seven years after she had arrived in New York, speaking no English and missing eight years of high-school education, she was awarded her doctorate in economics at the Binghamton campus of the State University of New York, which offered a high-quality economics programme.

My wife knew a lot about surviving hard times. So as soon as she left the bank, she did what came naturally to her, and working from our kitchen table, started thinking of commodities she could buy in China and sell in Europe. One day she asked me what ferrosilicon was. I had to look it up. Ferrosilicon is a naturally occurring substance added to raw steel to make the steel harder, heat resistant and more valuable. All steel makers need it, and they need it to be pure as possible. Ying had found a company in Wuhan, central China, that produced ferrosilicon, apparently of excellent quality.

Although in May 1989, Chinese student unrest was bubbling in Shanghai and Beijing, she decided she had to visit the company, and flew there via Hong Kong. When she arrived at her hotel, she found a message from her father: 'Don't come to Beijing. Something is going to happen.' It was 4 June 1989. The next day, Chinese Army units invaded Tiananmen Square — 'The Gate of Heavenly Peace' — and the world recoiled as reports came in of the clampdown, with one picture in particular, a tank steering left and right to avoid a student standing in front of it, becoming an icon of resistance to communist-style repression.

But Ying was made of stern stuff, and was undeterred by this newest wave of violence. She waited a few days, then flew to Wuhan, via Beijing. A truck from the factory met her at the airport and drove her for several hours on an unmade road. The factory had thought the events in Beijing had put an end to their hopes of a sale, and were delighted to see her. She was shown the furnace in which the ferrosilicon was extracted from the mined rock, and met the factory's leader, a typical Chinese entrepreneur with a background in metallurgy, who had found a way to exploit a naturally occurring, valuable resource She brought samples of the finished product back to London.

We had them tested, and it turned out that the producers were right: their product had virtually no impurities.

We were on to something, and needed help. My young cousin, aged twenty-three and just out of university, was looking for his first job, and we gave it to him: sitting in our London apartment, and finding a market amongst Europe's steel producers for the Chinese ferrosilicon. Before long, he had found two buyers. A few days later, he and I were in my car driving to factories in Germany, Luxembourg and Belgium. Terms were discussed, contracts were signed and we ordered the ferrosilicon from the Chinese. I had to buy the product in three forty-foot containers from the factory before I sold it to the European steelmakers. The containers would be shipped by barge down the Yangtse river to Shanghai, then taken by coastal vessel to the container port in Hong Kong, and then by ocean-going container vessel to Rotterdam, where they would be transferred onto Rhine barges and delivered to the steel manufacturers.

Now I had to turn my attention to financing the transactions. I went to see my bank in London. We had received letters of credit from the buyers in Belgium, Luxembourg and Germany, with which I would be paid once the product had arrived in their factories; however, my bank would not accept those credits as solid enough to finance the material I was going to buy from the Chinese. Undeterred, I transferred all the money I had into our business account to underwrite the transaction. I thought, now or never, and signed the letter of credit in favour of the Chinese company, payable three months following their shipment. I had to pay them in dollars, but before then, I would receive deutschemarks in payment from the European companies. I got around the currency mismatch by giving myself a margin of error for future currency movements. I hoped it was large enough. Then, we waited. Ying was confident that everything would work out. I was less sure, but comforted myself with a dose of fatalism: the die was cast, and the gods would decide.

Three weeks later my bank called me. The Chinese had presented their shipping documents to their bank in China. This meant that the ferrosilicon, which in its natural form looked like slate, had been mined, processed, sorted and cleaned, loaded into containers, and placed on a vessel bound for Europe. The Chinese bank would take my money three months later. Now we had to see if the product would arrive safely with our three customers in Europe, and if we would get paid.

Two months later I received a call from Belgium: 'The product is wet. The container was left open in Hong Kong. But we will pay because we want to see the quality.'

What a relief. Meanwhile the deutschemark, the currency which we received in payment, had strengthened somewhat against the dollar, so we made a currency profit. A lot of deutschemarks from Germany and Belgium arrived in my bank account. To remove any more currency risk, I changed most of them immediately into dollars to send as payment to the Chinese. The rest were our profit, and became pounds sterling. Our bank account swelled, and my bank manager asked me for a drink. I accepted, not having the heart to tell him that in three weeks, most of the money in my account would leave again, when the Chinese applied for payment from me under the letter of credit I had opened with them.

That was the point at which I decided to leave my job, give up my promising City career, and strike out into the unknown as an entrepreneur.

***

Have you ever gone skydiving? I have, long ago, in Hong Kong with some soldiers from my unit, when I was an army lieutenant. Poised on the edge of the exit from the small plane, you look down and try to remember what you were taught: 'Jump, count to three, then pull the cord that opens your parachute.' That's the hard bit. But with the soldiers watching you, there's only one way to go. It's an extraordinary feeling. You feel like a bird, released from your earthly bonds. You fall, the plane forgotten, the Earth spinning beneath. When you pull the cord the parachute jerks open, and you're floating. Suddenly — splat — you land in a paddy field, with silk billowing around you.

The first time you leave the safe corporate world and work for yourself, it's like skydiving. It's intimidating to wake that first morning and realise there's no monthly salary, no safety net beneath your feet. Then you remember all those meetings, mostly about nothing much, and the games you played with your colleagues and superiors, trying to get ahead. On your own, as an entrepreneur, your parachute is your own wit, wisdom, toil and tenacity, no more than that. Every day presents new and different challenges, but you must propel yourself forward, and keep getting things done.

There were so many things to do to get started, and I began flipping through my Rolodex. My friends were intrigued, and some were supportive. One of them, a solicitor at a famous City law firm, said he could help us set up the company. Then we had to find an accountant. I talked to someone I knew at one of the Big Four accounting firms, and realised I was out of my depth with them. So I went to the London telephone book, and looked in the Yellow Pages (remember those?). I found one who lived close by, and went to see him.

His office was on the first floor of a building with a Chinese restaurant beneath and consisted of two rooms, one of which held three or four men sitting at tables, their fingers tapping away at adding machines (remember *those*?), their other hands turning sheaves of documents. Mr Majainah, for that was his name, had his own office next door. He was small and bird-like, with bright eyes, and curious about how and why I had found him. Clearly, not many tall Englishmen walked into his office. I replied that I had a good experience of working with Indians in my City office, believed them to be intelligent and reliable, and thought his firm was probably much cheaper than a large accounting firm. He immediately corrected me, saying he was from Pakistan, not from India, but agreed with the rest of my comments. I explained my vision. He smiled, and asked me if I owned my flat. When I replied in the affirmative, he stood up, extended his hand and the deal was done.

A few years later I was prevailed upon, against my better judgment, to change Mr Majainah for another accountant. Afterwards, I regretted doing so. My first choice was correct. Mr Majainah was efficient, loyal, accurate, inexpensive, allowed me months to pay his invoices, and gave me excellent business advice, even about my investor. But more of that later.

Now we had a company, we had some revenue, and we even had a profit, albeit temporarily. What next? To start, we looked at various items we could buy from China and sell in Europe. Telephone modems, cashmere sweaters, shirts. It took me several weeks and a lot of argument to persuade the Chinese half of our team that our future did not lie in trading, because it required a lot of capital, and that whatever we traded in, there would always be someone else with more capital, who knew more than we did about a particular product line. We had been lucky with the ferrosilicon deal. Next time might be different.

I started to think of companies who could be interested in China, and who would listen to our story. While I researched the British corporate world for ideas, Ying flew to China, again via Hong Kong, and found friends or relatives who could help set up our office. She ended up establishing two — one in Shanghai and the other in Beijing — because she thought they were both important for what we would be trying to do. At the time, two offices felt very expensive, but time proved her right. Both offices became vital revenue and contact centres.

Another friend, who worked in a senior position for Rolls-Royce, the maker of aero-engines, told us the company needed independent help and advice in China, which they saw as a potentially important market. Rolls - Royce became active there in the mid-1970s, when the Chinese government bought a number of their engines and British Aerospace manufactured aeroplanes to mark the visit of British Prime Minister Edward Heath to China in 1973. The British engines had been left in their delivery crates in Xian, acquiring the name of 'terracotta warriors' amongst China's aviation professionals. Since the mid-1970s and this auspicious introduction, Rolls-Royce had sold a number of engines for the Boeing aircraft acquired by Air China, especially for the mid-range 757, for which Rolls-Royce was the preferred supplier. We signed a two-year contract to advise the head office in London on what was going on inside the aviation industry in China. Taking the advice of an acquaintance who had started a successful City financial advisory company, I persuaded Rolls-Royce to pay our retainer quarterly in advance. The cashflow improvement was significant, and our bank manager, who had begun to look gloomy, was impressed.

Our Beijing office needed a local, reputable company to support our application to open. John, our chosen representative, had worked for the large telephone operator American Telephone and Telegraph (AT&T) in

Beijing until June 1989, when virtually all the foreign companies who had arrived in China in the 1980s packed their bags and left, following the trouble in Tiananmen Square. John was well-connected enough to be able to find one of the largest Chinese state trading companies to sponsor us. I gave the London representative of this trading company an expensive dinner in a prestigious Mayfair based club. He was mostly silent throughout the meal, but a week later, our Chinese sponsorship was agreed. We rented a small office in Beijing's (and mainland China's) only modern office block at that time, the CITIC building, near the Forbidden City.

In Shanghai we turned to my wife's cousin, a man in his late forties who had worked as an electrical engineer most of his life. He had impressed me with his interest in a resurgent China when Ying and I had visited in 1988, and he was keen to join our little enterprise.

His first effort was to introduce us, late in 1989, to the Panda Radio factory in Nanjing, which wanted to enter the new business of making handsets for mobile telephones. The people at Nanjing Panda were interested in visiting England because they had heard of a British company near London, called Technophone that was a leading designer and manufacturer of soon to be popular portable mobile telephone handsets. They would pay their own travel and hotel costs, but needed someone to introduce them to the British company, and help them once they arrived. I accepted their request, which was made through my

Shanghai manager, to help them discuss a technology transfer deal.

We made contact with the factory. The first mobile networks in the world had originated in Scandinavia. In anticipation of the development of the British mobile phone market, the factory in Camberley, Surrey, had been set up in England by a Swede using Scandinavian technology.

Our first ever Chinese business delegation arrived at London's Heathrow from Nanjing via Shanghai, and we drove them to a hotel in nearby Windsor, a city famous for its royal castle, a few miles from the factory. It was the week before Christmas 1989, the moment when President Ceausescu and his wife were murdered by a Romanian mob in Bucharest. I shall never forget the look of dismay on the face of my English-speaking Chinese passenger as he listened to the report on my car radio of the events in Bucharest, which, I learned later, were to have a profound impact in Beijing.

When we took the delegation to visit Technophone their excitement, which had reached a high pitch, abated when they found that the machines used to manufacture the phones had been covered, to retain secrecy. Their interest in a joint venture was not reciprocated, and they left disappointed and empty-handed. (Technophone was acquired by the Finnish technology company Nokia in 1991, and formed an important leg in Nokia's world-conquering mobile phone strategy.)

All was not lost, however, because I learned something important from this visit: that mobile telephone networks, then small and expensive to use with large, heavy handsets, were the communications technology of the future. I envisioned that in a poor country like China, where fixed-line telephones were scarce, and limited to wealthy or well-connected individuals, mobile phone networks could meet a need for individuals and businesses to communicate easily and cheaply. I could imagine that China's huge population would eventually provide the largest single opportunity for mobile telephony. Here was a huge, untapped future growth market, which our Chinese visitors from Nanjing had already noticed. Wouldn't it be attractive for a foreign telecoms company to enter into a joint venture with a Chinese telephone operator to exploit this enormous opportunity?

I did some research on the Chinese mobile phone market. It had started, but was tiny, and was focused on the two principal cities of Beijing and Shanghai, with a thousand or two users in each city. The Chinese national fixed-line telephone company, China Telecom, was the sole mobile phone operator. Call costs were fixed by the Chinese government at a low rate. China Telecom was allowed to recover its investment in building the network by operating a monopoly business in selling handsets. These were imported from Europe, because the first mobile phone networks were built by the Swedish telecoms company Ericsson. European handsets, made by one of three or four companies, could be used, with modifications, on the Chinese Ericsson-built system. China Telecom sold them in China for around US$5,000 each, at a profit margin of more than 100% over the net imported price.

At this time, late in 1989, the British government had awarded two mobile-phone licences: one to Cellnet, a division of the monopoly British fixed-line operator, British Telecom; the other to a subsidiary of a leading electronics company, Racal. I contacted both companies. Cellnet told me that, in their view, China did not represent a viable operating market for mobile phone opportunities. Can you believe it? But at Racal Telecom I found a better reception, so to speak. The business development manager was enthusiastic and shared my vision. In June 1990 we drove to their headquarters, and met with him and his boss. He arranged for a visit to our Beijing office by a Racal Telecom representative in Hong Kong, a British territory since 1842, when China handed the island to Britain under the terms of the peace settlement that concluded the first opium war between the two countries. Ying flew to Beijing to meet him. By then British Airways had started a direct flight from London to Beijing and the Racal Telecom representative, (the father of Rory Stewart, the British Member of Parliament and former Minister of Prisons), turned out to be the retired head of the British Secret Service in the Far East, and working for whoever needed his Asian expertise. He gave us the all-clear and soon, Racal Telecom expressed their interest in working with us in China.

It was still early days for foreign companies in China, and telecoms was (and still is) a heavily restricted sector. We needed a local partner with enough power to push through a foreign joint venture. Our office in Shanghai contacted the city's mobile telephone operator. Always keen to be the first in China, the Shanghainese expressed an interest immediately. We introduced the two parties, and established communications. Our excellent relations with the Shanghai Telecoms people on the one hand, and with the leaders of Racal Telecom on the other enabled a common interest in exploiting China's future mobile phone market.

A few months after an exploratory visit to Shanghai in March 1991 had established a strong basis for Sino-British co-operation, the head of Racal Telecom, Gerry Whent (later Sir Gerry) led a team to Shanghai. Ying and our China team finalised an agreement between Racal Telecom and the Shanghai Telecoms operator for a joint venture that would train mobile operators all over China, and sell them discounted mobile-base-station equipment. This was possible because the advance of mobile phone technology, from analogue to digital, had overtaken Racal Telecom. Prevented by Chinese law from operating as a foreign telecoms operator in China's mobile phone market, Racal saw in China a market where they could sell, and realise some of the value, in their almost new but already obsolete analogue base-station equipment. For Racal, the alternative to selling the out of date equipment to Chinese mobile network operators was to write it off, much of it unused.

Racal Telecom were delighted with their new Chinese friends. But they warned us, their small executive team had become overstretched as they attempted to leverage their first-mover advantage in Britain into a global business. They would allocate a limited period of time to finalising the contact with the Chinese and obtaining the operating licence. After twelve months they would have to withdraw from the project, as they did not have the time and manpower to spend longer on what they regarded as an interesting, but ultimately non-essential project. We passed this message to the Shanghainese. Racal paid us a monthly retainer, plus a small equity share of the future project (if it happened). We crossed our fingers, and waited for the operating licence to be issued by the Shanghai telecom authorities. Meanwhile, Racal Telecom changed their name to Vodafone and planned their listing on the London stock market.

That was exciting, but we hardly stopped to celebrate as we were on to the next project.

In Beijing, the government had seen the need to establish the country's first modern retail store. The German airline Lufthansa was developing a commercial centre in western Beijing. It would contain a hotel, which the German hotel group, Kempinski, would operate, and a large shopping centre, which the Chinese wanted to turn into their first modern department store, to be called the YaoYi Shopping Centre (later well known to many expatriates who lived in Beijing since the mid-1990s). Our office there told us they had been approached by a local official to find a foreign investor with retail expertise, who would be interested in a joint venture.

The potential seemed obvious. I contacted the head office of leading British retailer Marks & Spencer. But they told me the events in Tiananmen Square a few months previously had placed China out of bounds for their company. They doubted that China would ever become a country with a modern retail industry. In any case, they were not interested. So we turned to another, much smaller and less well-known British retailer: Littlewoods, known mainly for operating an extremely profitable weekly football pools system. But Littlewoods also operated chain stores and mail-order shopping in northern England. I contacted their headquarters in Liverpool. A few days later, we were visited in London by an experienced Littlewoods executive. He returned to Liverpool convinced of our bona fides, and eager to convey the project's potential.

A month later, a Littlewoods team headed by a former McKinsey consultant visited Beijing, spent a month doing a feasibility study, and pronounced favourably. Littlewoods decided to go ahead, and signed an agreement to jointly work out a detailed plan for the shopping centre and to invest US$7 million to gain a 70 per cent majority share of the project, leaving the Chinese to find themselves the investment balance of US$3 million. Now we had two major projects in the pipeline.

Our Shanghai representative, Frank, had found a nice place to establish his office, in a centrally located colonial building that had been taken over by the government after 1949 as a formal residence and banqueting centre. Standing back from one of the city's main thoroughfares, it was surrounded by gardens and trees planted by its French builders seventy or so years before. As Frank moved in, he told us of a factory in nearby Anhui province that made oil and air filters for Chinese tractors, and which he thought would provide another opportunity. The German car producer Volkswagen, which had started a car-assembly joint venture in Shanghai in 1983, had been prevailed upon by its Chinese government partner, after lengthy discussions and much foot-dragging, to produce a modernised saloon designed specifically for the local Chinese market. They obliged, and called it the Santana 2000. The Shanghai Government, Volkswagen's partner in the joint venture, reciprocated by decreeing that Shanghai's taxis would all be Santanas. The vehicle's manufacture used locally produced components, up to a proportion of 90 per cent. The Bengbu Filter factory was looking for a company in Europe that could sell them the knowhow to make modern car filters, to be used by Chinese garages as the aftermarket replacements for worn-out originals fitted by Shanghai Volkswagen.

I discovered that Volkswagen's main European filter supplier was a company called Mann, based in southern Germany. They told me that the Bengbu company had already approached them, and they had quoted a price of several million dollars for the technology. This was some way beyond Bengbu's budget, and explained why the Chinese had turned to us. Further research uncovered a British company based in Plymouth, who when we approached them said they would be happy to sell their knowhow for a sum much smaller than Mann. Though the Chinese preferred Mann, as the original VW supplier, they acknowledged the need to compromise to suit their purse. They agreed to visit Plymouth in England to arrange a technology supply contract.

Several weeks later, a party of six Bengbu representatives arrived in London, consisting of the factory head, two factory technical assistants, the local manager of the state bank which was providing the finance, a senior member of the local government, and a contract negotiator from one of the government trading companies, which were at that time the only entities in China permitted to negotiate foreign contracts and exchange foreign currency.

After a night in a hotel in London, the Chinese delegation, together with me and an interpreter, travelled by train to Plymouth, where the negotiations took place. Here I was exposed for the first time to the famous Chinese negotiating process, involving tight-lipped silences, expressions of anger and disbelief, and long delays; however, after a week of discussions a contract was concluded, whereby a sum of around US$400,000 would be paid in stages to the British company in return for filter designs and training assistance. Our share was US$40,000, which we would receive in stages over the following two years of the project's life. To put this in context: at that time you could buy a one-bedroomed apartment in an unfashionable part of London for this amount, and a 150 ml glass of Chardonnay in London cost two dollars. But even before we paid ourselves, our company overheads, with three offices to support, were running up to $250,000 and more (nearly the price of a mansion in the home counties at the time). I had invested my savings in the company, and although our bank manager had helped us secure a small business loan from the government, anyone who has started a new business, particularly one that needs scale early on, will know the value of every new item of revenue that comes along. It was an important development.

In the space of two years I had married, visited China, and entered a new world. My fear of failing was neutralised by exhilaration, and the fascination of discovering what lay beyond the Great Wall of China, and even more, by discovering our reserves of energy, ingenuity and self-belief. Joyfully, I discarded some of the aspects of myself that had been useful in my previous career, like organisational conformity and careful attention to my superiors' whims. Now, Ying and I were the organisation, with both employees and clients looking to us for ideas and direction. This bolstered my confidence, and released the enormous amounts of energy I would need to successfully forge the path I had chosen. I realised what people meant when they talked about the social and economic importance of the entrepreneur's imagination and dynamism. But newly married and with a new enterprise in a field I still knew little about, had I bitten off more than I could chew?

II

SUBMARINES AND SPIES

I had delayed visiting our China offices because I had plenty to do in London with the start-up, and was focused on developing the revenue stream that would kick off our business. But by early 1991, I thought I could delay the visit to China no longer. After all, China was the essential part of our business, and much depended on the efforts of our people there. A strong, trusting relationship between us in London and our Chinese staff thousands of miles away would be a key factor in our success. True, my wife was Chinese, and she formed the essential link between China and London, corresponding by fax or telephone every day with our Chinese colleagues. But I thought that I should strengthen the link by making myself better known to our Chinese workers.

So, in April, I bought an economy class return ticket to Beijing. I boarded the plane looking forward to meeting the people we were working with, and to a trip north to Harbin in Heilongjiang province, near the Chinese border with Siberia, to visit China's largest oilfield, Daqing, because we had been approached to help the local refinery purchase components in Europe.

Since my Chinese honeymoon in late spring 1988, travel from London to China had become easier. British Airways had opened a direct flight to Beijing from London Heathrow, and that was the one I took. Beijing airport in 1991 was the size of a small regional airport in Europe or the United States today. We didn't have to carry our baggage from the plane ourselves, as we did later in Shanghai, but there was only one baggage conveyor inside the terminal.

I was met at the airport exit by John, our smiling office manager, complete with a typed itinerary, a refinement he had learned from his previous time as China manager for America's phone operator AT&T. John had insisted on hiring an office car, with a driver. He explained that travelling from our office in central Beijing to see Chinese clients in and around the city was not served by the Beijing subway system, and taxis were expensive and unreliable. He did not say, but I guessed, that operating a car and driver gave our company the prestige and standing, in a country in which private car ownership was still rare, that would enable Chinese clients to trust us. So I demurred to John, although the cost added thousands of dollars to our overhead. The airport road, although narrow and tree-lined, was unusually well-paved, and I remarked on this to John, who was sitting beside me in the back seat. He explained that the airbase used by China's leaders was near the civil airport, and they also needed to use this road.

Looking out of the car window to either side, I was struck by the barren countryside, which looked like a moonscape. Yet every now and again beside the road a village appeared, populated by small mud or brick houses surrounded by fields of maize, some chickens and pigs, and a few trees. There were hardly any cars, but we passed people riding bicycles, and as we approached Beijing, larger office buildings began to appear. We reached the outer ring-road, at that time the third (there are now seven ring-roads around Beijing). With it appeared the large Soviet-era buildings that then defined China's municipal architecture, broken up with one or two newly built office blocks which continued to be based on variations of the massive Soviet communist style. A year later, a local real estate developer in Beijing made a huge splash by hiring an Italian firm of architects to design a beautiful steel and glass office building, known as Silver Tower, visible for a mile or two to traffic approaching the much used junction of the third ring road with the airport road. This building was the poster child of stylish modern architecture not just in Beijing, but in China, and it's still there. Modern Beijing building design acts as a metaphor for the post-Deng evolution of Chinese society and its economy: a compromise between conservative instructions issued by the city's planning department, which result in practical, ugly buildings, and highly imaginative modern buildings designed first by foreign, and now by home-grown Chinese architects.

An hour later, we reached Beijing's main street, Jianguomen, an avenue running west to east which divides the capital into north and south, and separates the emperor's palace, the Forbidden City, from the rest of Beijing, which was originally laid out on a north-south axis, like the ancient Chinese capital of Chang'an and the old Japanese imperial city, Kyoto. To position the main building facing south was an important part of the ancient Chinese system known as 'feng shui' (literally 'wind, water').

On either side of this thoroughfare, small streets could be seen leading into alleys built up on either side with wooden homes, each of them laid out traditionally around a courtyard. These were the famous 'hutongs', where John Fairbank, the distinguished professor of Chinese at Harvard University for several decades after the Second World War, had lived in the 1930s with his American wife. According to him and others, life in the hutongs fosters a strong sense of community, with everyone looking after each other and knowing each other's secrets, likes and dislikes, daily routines and family histories, for better or worse.

There were no cars in these narrow alleyways, only a few bicycles. Children played in the streets, residents gathered to gossip and sometimes sat out to drink or smoke. Such was hutong life, which sounded an ideal way to live in a large city. But by the time I arrived many of the hutongs had been knocked down, and others were being demolished. Much of inner Beijing looked like a building site. This, of course, was progress.

A few years later an inspired Beijing official, with prompting from concerned foreigners, managed to call a halt to the hutong destruction. Now, thanks to such intervention, a few of the ancient streets remain, many of them near Tiananmen Square and the Forbidden City. One of these hutong houses, complete with its courtyard and heavy wooden front gate, now has rarity value and commands a higher price than a townhouse in Manhattan or central London, or a 'foyer' in Paris. Very few are still lived in by the families who inhabited them fifty years ago. With their newly built gates, freshly painted front doors, wire-topped walls and electronic alarm systems, they are owned, and sometimes lived in as well, by Chinese real-estate or hi-tech tycoons, or businessmen from Hong Kong or Taiwan.

The hutongs were interspersed with factories, from which belched smoke from the coal used everywhere then in China for heat and energy. China has the largest coal reserves of any country in the world, much of which is easily recoverable from shallow mines. Unfortunately, the coal quality is poor, often more like lignite, and highly polluting. In 1991, large factories employing many thousands of people, and making everything from shirts to bicycles, operated in the centres of Beijing and Shanghai. The largest of these in Beijing was a huge steel factory, later moved to a location hundreds of miles outside of the city. Enterprising developers, far-sighted enough to anticipate the future demand for quality offices in central locations, were already co-operating with local officials to take some of these factories over, and convert them into office accommodation. (By 2010 or earlier, all these factories had either closed down or been moved elsewhere. Private accommodation blocks would have to wait a few years, until the Chinese could afford to buy them. In 1991, no one in China had any money, and everyone lived in housing owned by the government.)

After checking into my hotel, a French-Chinese joint venture that was then the only Western style hotel in the city centre, I was taken to our office, on the sixth floor of an imposing glass-fronted building nearby, where I met all three of our other employees. One, in his fifties, was a retired officer from the Chinese Air Force, whom we had hired to help us with our advisory work for Rolls-Royce. Another was a young woman, bilingual in English and Chinese, who had worked for several years for a large Chinese trading company. The third, tall and pretty, had been hired by John to be his office manager's assistant (and then his girlfriend, as I learned later from my Chinese wife, who was, of course, privy to the social network that existed inside our office). They were as interested to meet me as I was to meet them. My wife had told me that eating together was an essential Chinese way of initiating and cementing relationships, so after we had had a chat, I took the team out to a delicious lunch in a nearby restaurant, where our discussions continued. Our office manager, John, had spent several years in the United States, and had acquired a business degree from Buffalo, in the State of New York, so he was easily able to translate back and forth.

The following morning, I discovered that the hired car, a large Mercedes saloon, had been placed at my disposal. It was one of the very few in Beijing, and initially I queried the cost; however, I decided not to object to it, as I knew that appearances in China mean everything. I didn't want to get off on the wrong foot with our office staff, and — after all — it was only for a day. If John, our Beijing manager, thought that I needed a Mercedes to impress our clients, then I would go along with him. One of the meetings this car took me to was with the young, Oxford-educated Guo Shuqing, reputed even then to be a future star within the government. Over lunch we discussed the Chinese railway system. He was extremely polite, and listened carefully to my description of British Rail and its shortcomings. Today, he is the head of the Chinese bank regulator in Beijing and a senior member of the Chinese Government. In late 2017 Guo was considered for the new governor of the Chinese Central Bank. That job went to Yi Gang, another of our friends from those early days, who, in 1990 as a young economics professor, wrote an article for our publication *China Monthly Review*.

Looking back to that period early in 1991, it seems hard to believe today that the issue of China's economic and social development, which has since transformed the world, was still in the balance. But after the clampdown of 5 June 1989 in Beijing, it was.

Mao Tse Tung, the leader who had brought the Communists to power in China in 1949, ruled the country until his death in April 1976. The power struggle that followed Mao's death was won in 1978 by Deng Xiaoping, one of Mao's early henchmen, and one of the few leaders who had not been sent to his grave as an ageing Mao struggled viciously to hold onto power. Deng, a longstanding party member and participant in the famous Long March, had first emerged as a senior Chinese leader in the early 1960s. His long experience near the top of the Chinese Communist Party, and as a close associate of Mao, meant that he knew where all the levers of Chinese political power were located. Deng's insights and vision, coupled with his hard-won prestige within the party, allowed him to turn the country's focus towards reform, and to looking outwards.

China's first steps towards change encouraged foreign multinationals like the German car company, Volkswagen, to invest in the country via joint ventures. In the early 1980s the economy began to grow, stimulated especially by investment from overseas Chinese based in Taiwan, Hong Kong, Singapore and elsewhere in Asia.

Deng's economic vision was matched on the political front by his protégé, Prime Minister Zhao Ziyang, who started to speak of experimenting with forms of government based on suffrage and representation. But as demand increased and price inflation rose through the 1980s the Chinese political atmosphere became increasingly charged. In the late 1980s students, first in

Beijing, then in other major Chinese cities, started to take to the streets to demonstrate their support for representative government. Deng was ready to take a risk to spark change and stimulate economic growth, but even he became alarmed when thousands of students marched from Peking University to Beijing's central square and occupied the huge and now iconic Tiananmen Plaza located next to the massive Congress Hall, opposite the former imperial palace known as the Forbidden City and... Mao's mausoleum. A state visit in early June 1989 by reforming Soviet Prime Minister Mikhail Gorbachev coincided with an escalation in the student demonstrations and threatened the party's sense of control. Deng, alarmed, and made furious by the loss of face, used his position as head of the Chinese Army to order Chinese soldiers from elite regiments based near Beijing to remove the demonstrators.

The Communist Party leadership was shocked by the unrest and the clampdown. The emphasis turned to stability and preservation. Reform stopped. Deng placed Prime Minister Zhao Ziyang under house arrest, and appointed Jiang Zemin, from Shanghai, as a puppet president, with the hard line conservative Li Peng as prime minister. For many, it looked like the end of a brief China spring. Most foreign companies who had arrived in China to investigate the opportunities packed their bags and returned home.

Considering this backdrop, my conversation with Guo Shuqing was confined to pleasantries, his reticence probably due to the fact that China was still under a cloud of shock and conservative reaction. Hard-liners dominated the government, and abroad China's foreign relations were in deep freeze. The new president, Jiang Zemin, lacked the power or indeed the will to restart the programme of reform and change.

But the business atmosphere in Beijing was not entirely frozen. Economic momentum had spilled over from the period of fast growth in the early 1980s. People had not forgotten. And though the government's official position was static, it was made clear to me from the meetings I had that some thought this period of deep-freeze would end, and that change would resume, although no one could predict when.

The following day it was back to the airport for a local Air China flight to Harbin. John travelled with me. The aircraft was one of the four-engine jets made by British Aerospace, with Rolls-Royce engines, which the Chinese government had resuscitated from their years of storage. The small plane was cramped, noisy and filled to the gills. After two hours we reached a place that looked like Russia, a near neighbour only a few miles away. Harbin is famous in China for two things: an ice city, created each winter (temperatures there can reach minus thirty degrees centigrade), and second, the Harbin accent, a kind of Received Pronunciation which enabled the city to supply a large proportion of television newsreaders. But it was springtime when I visited, and my then untutored ear could not distinguish the local dialect.

We stayed the night in a local hotel, opposite a Russian Orthodox church, and not far away from a nightclub, outside which statuesque Russian blondes encouraged passing trade to join them in festivities. The next morning, we were met after breakfast by a Daqing representative, fluent in English. We transferred to his car, and drove for several hours westwards along a tarmacked road to the Daqing oil field, which was at that time responsible for most of China's oil production, and famous throughout the country as one of one of Communist China's earliest industrial achievements. Apart from occasional Russian churches, we saw flat, bleak expanses of open countryside. Soon we started to pass oil wells, each one marked with a nodding donkey. In Daqing itself we found shops, modern apartment blocks, sports pitches, a bustling main street and a large, modern hotel into which we decamped.

Our hosts were the Daqing purchasing office. At the dinner that followed our arrival, I remember drinking most of a bottle of the famous and expensive Chinese liquor called Maotai, as the faces of the five Chinese who were our hosts became redder and redder, until they were unable to drink any more. I think they were hoping that I would slide slowly under the table. Fortunately, my time as a soldier had hardened me to excessive amounts of alcohol, and I felt no serious ill-effects either on the night or the morning after. Chinese liquor, at 60 per cent proof, contains more alcohol than Western spirits, but is distilled to exclude the impurities that make several glasses of whisky or even beer likely to give many people some kind of morning after effect. This big night out cemented our relationship, which proved to be robust and financially successful.

The following morning, we started back in the car to Harbin, where we would catch a flight to Shanghai via a short stopover in Beijing. One event that occurred on the way sticks in my memory. A motorcycle, passing at right-angles to our road, jumped the lights we were approaching, and was hit by a car travelling at speed towards us. The man riding the cycle was literally cut in half. I shall never forget the lower part of his head and jawbone, which had been split in two, rolling along the road towards us. The traffic slowed and stopped, as it always does when a serious accident occurs. We had to stop, and the Chinese man sitting beside me was immediately sick out of the rear window. Then we had to wait, while the police and emergency crews arrived to start clearing the debris, including several cars that had become involved. A fire truck arrived, uncoiled its hose and started spraying a powerful jet of water on the tarmac to remove the pools of blood. Eventually the police waved the traffic on, and we started to move again.

This sticks in my memory as a symbol of how China was at that time: a poor, undeveloped society confronting the forces of change, without the means to control or master them. China's early drivers took the most rudimentary tests to get a licence, and were in a hurry to get everywhere. Severe road accidents were common, and road fatalities soared. It took decades for Chinese driving regulations and policemen to catch up with the rapid increase in automobile use.

Shanghai in 1991 was undeveloped, and unrecognisable as the cosmopolitan city it is today. Its prosperous, racy past in the interwar years had caught up with it when the Communist Party took over in 1949 and it was transformed into a model of communist endeavour, under the thumb of the central government in Beijing. On the famous Bund — the road along the river comparable to, say, the Left Bank of Paris — its empire-style buildings overlook the river, reflecting shadows of pre-war prosperity. Bicycles were everywhere, all travelling from home to factory in the morning rush-hour, and then back the other way in late afternoon. Large factory buildings, most of which emitted clouds of noxious smoke from dawn to dusk, as in Beijing, covered much of the city. Trees lined some of the roads, and an occasional cinema could be found on the street corners, near tea and cake shops. This had been the French quarter when Shanghai was a treaty port. Now, though, the impression was of depression, not particularly encouraging for someone like me who was betting on China's economic resurgence.

My wife's mother was Shanghainese, and Ying was determined to locate one of our offices here. She said the city would be reborn, because the Shanghainese were the most avaricious and commercially successful people in China. How right she was. The following year, 1992, was when Supreme Leader Deng Xiaoping encouraged

Shanghai to develop the large tract of farmland on the southern side of the Huangpu river called Pudong. When I first visited the city, Pudong had only a customs house and one or two other nondescript buildings. Today, Pudong contains three of the tallest buildings in Asia. Deng Xiaoping gave the Shanghainese their head, and they galloped away.

In Shanghai I met our local representative, who was fifteen years older than his colleague in Beijing. He had a professorial air about him which was accentuated by his thick black glasses. Our office in the Xingguo Guest House was in the centre of the French quarter, situated on the ground floor of a former colonial mansion, which had in pre-war years been the home of the head of one of the large British trading companies. It was surrounded by a lawn with handsome, mature acacia trees, and was encircled by a high brick wall, beyond which would have been heard the drone of traffic if there had been any cars or buses. But in 1991 there were only the relatively peaceful sounds of tinkling bicycle bells, the murmur of pedestrians and the occasional yell of local hawkers selling delicious hot steamed buns known in Chinese as baozi. As in Beijing, at this early stage of our business I found I had to simplify and modify my conversations with our local staff, who had all been operating previously in a world where no one really did much productive work, but everyone got paid enough in government-produced currency to eat and pay their rent. A kind of basic income, as it were. The number of foreign enterprises in Shanghai then was probably no more than five or ten, a tiny fraction of the number of state owned factories.

Over bottomless cups of tea, we discussed developments in London and how the Shanghai office, with its four staff members, could help us develop a client base. Our manager, who used the English name Frank, had worked all his life in a state owned electrical engineering company. He had no experience of modern business but he was intelligent, eager to succeed, and firmly believed in China's future as a dynamic economy, unlikely though that seemed. He suggested that some local state owned companies were keen to acquire foreign technology, particularly in the automotive sector, but in many other areas, too. I encouraged him to reach out around Shanghai, and send to us in London details of what they needed help with. I felt the need to remind him and his colleagues that we were a business, financed out of my own pocket. We had to generate revenue, and at some point, profits. They weren't working for the Chinese state any more.

I established a simple accounting system for financing our China offices, which were, at this stage, cost centres. Following an initial deposit of cash to allow furnishing and rent deposits, the system required that monthly cash advances would be sent from London to Shanghai and Beijing against monthly accounts completed by each office and then sent to London by fax, which itemised expenditure and showed starting and finishing bank balances. We operated the system successfully for a number of years without any mishaps. I believe that both office managers behaved in a fundamentally honest way, although when they could see that the business was generating significant amounts of revenue collected by London they did start to wonder, as the entrepreneurial Chinese will, whether they should be working for themselves rather than for us. From them I learned another important lesson: Chinese people want to work for themselves, and regard salaried work mainly as a learning and cash-saving experience, a preparation for some time in the future when they can become their own boss. I believe now that it is this characteristic that has made China the enormous and dynamic economy it is today. Any Chinese employee under the age of sixty who is still working for you after two years has probably already set up a business on the side, which he or she runs in the evening and at weekends (and probably also during working hours).

In the case of our Shanghai office, I was interested to see that one of our new employees was a well-presented young Chinese man of about thirty, speaking perfect English, who had previously been working for the local government. My office manager explained that this young man had been specially recommended by a friend in the all-important local government. Our manager believed him to be a spy, with the job of reporting on everything we were doing to the local police intelligence chief. He told me it was much better to keep the young man spying in our office, in order to have the co-operation of the local government. I agreed with him.

***

After a morning spent in the pleasant office with its high colonial corniced ceiling and heavy varnished wooden doors, I thought it would be interesting, if not particularly stimulating from a business perspective, to visit some local factories. One of these manufactured inflatable rubber dinghies, which were sold to the Chinese military. When we arrived, we found a number of male workers sitting or lying about smoking and drinking tea in various attitudes of repose. The dinghies were grey or brown, and looked unreliable. The factory owner said they wished to develop an export business to Europe and America. I gave the sample dinghies a brief inspection before telling them, in order to make my escape, that I would think about it. Another factory, called Shanghai Number 3 Radio Factory, made a great effort to welcome me and to show me around. They, too, wished to develop an export business, and were looking for a radio company in Europe with whom they could team up. They produced simple two-way radios which I tested by having a member of my team talk to me standing on the floor below. The radios worked. I said I would look for a suitable business partner for them in Europe after I had returned home.

Unlikely as it may sound, the visit to Shanghai Number 3 Radio Factory was in fact the beginning of a spectacularly interesting and rather lucrative business which we managed to develop over the course of the next year or two. I did follow through on my promise to them after my return home, by attending a radio communications exhibition at Earl's Court, a huge exhibition centre in London. There, I met a British company that was particularly proud of one of their products: submarine communications equipment. From their representatives, I learned how important it was for submarines to remain submerged, therefore hidden, while communicating by radio with their headquarters, which could be thousands of miles distant. Such communication was made possible by a very long wavelength that could travel through water and over very long distances. Only a handful of countries in the world possessed this technology. China was not one of them. Perhaps there might be an opportunity for them, with their special technology, to co-operate with us, with our local offices and know-how in China.

I went to the library and I found an up-to-date copy of *Jane's Fighting Ships*, a large, illustrated reference manual I knew about, because as a child I had been passionately interested in armies, aircraft and warships. There, I found a whole page on the Chinese Navy complete with the information I was looking for: China possessed about 200 diesel-powered submarines. Clearly, there was a market in China for submarine communications. My next task was to visit the radio company's headquarters in Sussex.

Several months later, a two-man team from the British radio company flew out to Hong Kong. Accompanied by our office staff, they started their presentations in

Shanghai, then went to Wuhan (the site of the Chinese Navy communications research centre) and finished in Beijing. At each presentation, a small man sat in the middle of the front row of the audience. A day or two after the last presentation, when the sales team from Sussex were on their way to the airport, the small man presented himself to our office. It transpired that he was the senior officer from the Chinese Navy charged with overall responsibility for their submarine communications research, and he was very interested in our British company.

Before long, a delegation from China arrived to visit our client at the headquarters in Sussex, England. The team included a Chinese professor who had spent twenty years researching the science of underwater radio transmissions. Since the 1970s, the Chinese had attempted to develop their own underwater communications system and had got most of the way, but were missing the final algorithms. They had approached another, much larger British company, Marconi, but something had gone wrong with the relationship, and our much smaller client now had an opportunity. That was our good fortune, because Marconi was a powerful and aggressive competitor. (Note: this British company had an Italian name because the inventor Guglielmo Marconi had established the world's first radio factory in Essex, England in 1898 after receiving a British patent for his technology.)

Because the British Navy was an important client, our British company had several retired naval officers on its staff. Assisted by some strong liquor, it wasn't long before the international language of naval veterans overcame Anglo-Chinese cultural and language barriers. After a week of discussions that were intermediated and translated by our personnel from Beijing, the Chinese delegation were sent home with hangovers, leaving behind a signed memorandum of intent which promised substantial equipment purchases over the following two or three years. Our financial share of this single deal amounted to about a calendar year of our total annual running costs.

Thus it was that smiling fortune had turned my apparently inconsequential visit to a rundown Shanghainese radio factory into the real promise of a large Anglo-Chinese radio equipment contract. However, we had a major hurdle to leap over — an export licence for radio equipment and knowhow developed in Britain that would be used by the Chinese Navy. This seemed to me to be a major obstacle to the consummation of the contract. Our client, the Sussex company that had much experience in these matters, assured me that getting an export licence from the NATO sensitive technology agency COCOM would be relatively straightforward. It took a couple of months, but they were right. The deal was approved by COCOM, and consisted of a series of shipments of radio receivers that would be fitted into the Chinese submarines, plus radio-drive units — or transmitters — which would be located on land in the relevant naval bases, plus instruction and training to take place in Sussex over a two-week period. In total, the Chinese bought 200 long-wave receivers and six long-wave transmitters. The whole transaction took place over a period of about two years.

In the middle of this happy event, as we concluded the deal, I received a telephone call from someone calling himself 'Mr Brown', who said he worked for the Foreign Office and wished to see me. His office turned out to be in Admiralty Arch, the tall building that separates Pall Mall from Trafalgar Square in London — now converted into a luxury hotel. As soon as I sat down in front of Mr Brown, I realised that the man behind the desk in front of me was probably not called Mr Brown and was not from the Foreign Office at all. His tone was unfriendly. He started by telling me that his organisation had received worrying reports of submarine radio equipment being provided to 'our enemies, the Chinese'. Apparently I had instigated this business, which obviously ran counter to British interests, and I might also have transgressed the relevant regulations governing trade with hostile powers. Could I explain myself?

I replied by confirming that his information was correct, but that the relevant export licences had been obtained from COCOM, and therefore the question of legality did not arise. I was then treated to a ten-minute harangue by 'Mr Brown' on my naivety and the regrettable nature of this transaction. Was I aware, 'Mr Brown' asked, that a young Chinese graduate from Imperial College whom I had hired in our London office was in fact working for Chinese intelligence, with the job of reporting all our activities to the Chinese government?

I said I did not know this, but added that setting up and operating a business assisting British companies to develop trade and exports would be interpreted by many as a patriotic thing to do. 'Mr Brown' sniffed, warned me that the matter was under investigation and that I may be contacted again, but that I was free to go, 'for the time being'.

I had spent long enough in the military to be able to see through the harsh tones to the reality underneath, that the British intelligence services were miffed that our transaction with China had slipped through their net. But the horse had already bolted, and there was nothing much they could do now except try to frighten me and express their frustration. I never heard any more of the matter. Still, the incident made me realise that our work had assumed a certain national importance. It was sobering to think that we were being watched by the intelligence services from at least two countries.

III

MOVING FORWARD, BUT NOT IN A STRAIGHT LINE

Our leap of faith seemed to be paying off. In a period of about one year, we had secured major British companies as advisory clients in China, and had arranged a technology transfer contract between a Chinese and a British company. The downside was that a London office and two China offices, with ten personnel in total spread between the three locations, had pushed me to my financial limit. My bank manager advised me to sell some equity in the business to an investor who could share some of the risk and financial burden in return for sharing in the company's potential. In late 1990, China's profile amongst Western companies still suffered from the negative shockwaves which had been transmitted by the brutal suppression of Tienanmen Square in June 1989. On the other hand, our progress as a business seemed to me to be strong enough to be able to persuade an adventurous investor to participate in our enterprise at an acceptable price.

I turned from negotiating contracts and marketing, to writing an investment proposal, and quickly realised that my other responsibilities as chief marketer, negotiator, organiser and financial officer, not to mention husband, would not allow me to complete an attractive document in a month or so. I needed an experienced mind working alongside me, to produce a pitch which would attract and persuade someone who was looking to invest a sum of one or two hundred thousand pounds in a project which could provide returns of many times over a multi-year period.

Once again, luck was on my side. With a couple of weeks, through friends, I had found and met a financial expert who was experienced in helping small start-ups like our company to raise equity capital from external investors. Within a month or two, we had completed a marketing document for our business. It was aimed at private wealthy investors (known in the venture capital world as 'angels'), and we placed it in a specialist magazine devoted entirely to finding investors for early stage companies. I didn't have long to wait. Within a couple of weeks I had received two separate, credible approaches to discuss investing in our company.

One was from a syndicate of middle-aged bankers from the City, who had pooled their bonuses into a substantial sum, part of which they wished to invest in an early stage business. The other was from an individual who had already backed several start-ups with some success. Both wanted to invest in our young company. After a series of meetings, I chose the experienced investor over the younger bankers, on the basis that he could provide our business not just with the capital we needed, but with useful advice on the many issues faced by a young and growing business.

A surprising thing happened a few days before we met to conclude the shareholding agreement in our office, which we had moved from our apartment to two rooms above an antique shop in Westbourne Grove in London. Ying and I visited our new investor at his home in the country. We met his wife, had supper and stayed the night in his house, returning to London the following day. Over dinner, his wife commented that her husband had had a Chinese girlfriend while he was an undergraduate at university. She said that she believed that his main motivation for investing in our business was because he liked Chinese ladies. Her husband made no comment, and changed the subject.

It was difficult to know whether to take this remark seriously, and to judge whether it should have any impact on our decision to allow this individual to participate in our business. Our several previous meetings with this individual had covered a total of at least six hours. I had made some separate inquiries about him from professionals who had worked previously with him. He came across as an experienced, successful, tough, but reasonable individual — the kind of person that many entrepreneurs would like to have backing them. We proceeded with the investment agreement. A few days later our ownership of the company had been reduced to seventy per cent, but we had received £40,000 in our bank account, with the promise of £160,000 more to follow. Two hundred thousand pounds for thirty per cent of our business seemed a very fair price to pay for a secure financial foundation, although there was also the possibility of the investor being able to increase his shareholding if he decided to, and under certain conditions. I pushed the warning we had received from the investor's wife to the back of my mind.

Her words resurfaced when, a month or two later, we had started a new transaction which involved a Scottish pump manufacturer selling technology, through our company, to two Chinese factories in different parts of China. I thought it would be wise to familiarise our investor with the kind of transactions we were doing, and I suggested that he join my partner Ying on a trip to Glasgow, to visit the Scottish company. Ying told me over supper that on her return late in the afternoon from the trip, as they sat side by side in the commuter plane, the investor had surprised her by placing his hand on her knee. Suspecting what this implied, she quickly told him that she was married, and was not interested in any extra-marital activity.

The words a month or two earlier from the wife of the investor returned to my mind. I thought quickly that it was probably not too late to get in touch with the banker syndicate who had expressed their investing interest, some months earlier. On the other hand, could I really believe that a reputable and experienced investor, more than a decade older than I, could think of endangering a project in which he had agreed to invest serious money with such behaviour? I decided to give him the benefit of the doubt, said nothing, and let the matter pass.

This turned out to be a serious mistake. The following year, soon after our investor had raised his interest in our company to 51%, he took me aside, and told me that on his recent trip to visit our offices in China, he had started an affair with the pretty office assistant, and former girlfriend, of our Beijing representative. He asked me to arrange the transfer of this girl from Beijing to our London office. It was not difficult for me to refuse his request, or to tell him that if he wanted to pursue extra-marital relations with women, it was his business, but he should do so outside his business relations with us. Needless to say, when I told my wife and business partner of this conversation, she was disgusted, reminding me of what had happened in the flight to Glasgow, and of what the investor's wife had said a year or so previously.

I felt like one of the main characters in a business school case, faced by an apparently insoluble challenge to which, nevertheless, somewhere there was a good response. I wondered what the clever answer was. Was it possible to dismiss a majority shareholder for misconduct? I turned to two trusted senior relatives who advised me that as the investor effectively controlled the company, I had no choice but to soldier on. I took their advice. (Years later, a lawyer told me what the clever answer was: I should have brought a case of gross misconduct against the investor and sought damages from him for bringing the company into disrepute, which appeared in a clause in his service contract with the company.) In today's world of zero-tolerance of female harassment and female inequality in the workplace, this kind of behaviour seems incredible. Younger people may not realise that things used to be very different from what they are today. But three or four decades ago, it was common to see women being mistreated and abused in the workplace, and it was truly rare to find a woman in a senior corporate position. Those who were in such positions often had to tolerate condescension, smutty comments and even physical advances and threats from male colleagues. All of these manifestations were regarded as normal in most large companies. Although I felt, personally, that our investor had stepped over a red line by trying to force me to bring his girlfriend from China nearer to his home in England, I doubted that, given how people treated such behaviour at that time, many other people would see it the way I did. Certainly the investor's attitude confirmed my view.

Naturally, I bitterly regretted allowing our investor to acquire a majority control of our business. My accountant had told me early on that, in his opinion, we should not have allowed the investor to buy shares in our company, because 'something' told him there was something wrong with him. I should have listened to his instincts. Today, I regret not taking the legal advice which would have led to our investor's dismissal, and presumably, significant damages being paid by him to us. My failure to cut out the destructive element from the company poisoned the relationship between us founders, and our investor. Over the following two years, I spent much of my time trying to find a way to replace him as an investor with a more appropriate person or institution.

***

Meanwhile, my wife had become pregnant, and in May 1992, our first child was born. Anyone who is a parent will know what a difference our daughter's arrival made to our household. But at the same time, it changed my risk appetite. An appetite for achievement when it's impossible to know what the future holds makes an entrepreneur into a risk-taker. Success depends on making good judgments, as well as luck. Sometimes, though, events don't work out as well as you wanted or expected. Then you have to call on all your survival instincts. Having young dependents changes your mind's calculus. Where previously you were comfortable with tolerating the worst possible case because the upside possibility was so exciting, now you tend to seek safety and avoid danger. This is not a helpful change of vision for someone running a fast-growing business which is still in an early stage of evolution, because you have to be alert every day to taking opportunities before they disappear, and invariably these opportunities bring risks with them.

In fact, though, our business was accelerating. Our Shanghai office had discovered a rich seam of activity in assisting European auto parts companies to sell technology to Chinese factories. Many of these companies wanted to become suppliers to the large and growing car production joint venture which Volkswagen had established in Shanghai in 1983, and which now dominated the baby Chinese car market. Typically, we would receive from our office in Shanghai a new requirement for a machine or a technology which had been received by them through their relationship network from one or other auto parts factory in or near Shanghai. This might involve grinding surfaces to very high specifications, or machining an engine part. All required a high level of technical expertise which could be found in one of the countries which produced high-specification machine tools — mainly Japan and Germany, sometimes Switzerland (expensive but very high quality), France, Italy or the UK. After clarifying the engineering requirement and the approximate budget, we searched for possible suppliers. We searched worldwide, but mainly in Europe, for two reasons: it was easier to deal with companies based in countries which we could easily visit, and Volkswagen always sourced their own parts from European suppliers, usually German ones. This made it much easier for the Chinese supplier to sell their machined parts either to the joint venture in Shanghai for new cars, or as replacement parts.

It was a good idea to visit a company in person when we first made contact with them, to persuade them of our competence and bona fides, while we could check whether they had the technical competence, commercial flexibility and desire to win a contract against stiff international competition. Doing business with a Chinese company can try the patience, and requires a flexible approach and an appetite for something new. Sometimes a European company we approached told us they did not want to share their technology with the Chinese, for fear of imitation. Or we would be rejected because they already knew of the opportunity, or had exclusive sales representatives in China or elsewhere in Asia. Normally, though, our approaches were received with interest, and it was unusual for companies to reject our demand for a fee of ten percent on the value of any sale which was brought to them by us and negotiated with our help.

Other transactions followed the car filter transaction described in chapter II. The Beijing based Chinese trading company who had handled the car filter transaction was pleased with our ability to locate sources of European technology, and equally important, to persuade the companies involved to enter into technology transfer discussions with the Chinese companies who wanted to acquire and use the technology. In those pre-internet days, a facsimile from a Chinese company, written in imperfect English (or French or German or Italian), arriving unannounced in the middle of the night or early morning, with a proposal of 'co-operation' often did not receive very much attention. By contrast, a telephone call, followed up by a visit in person, from a reputable and well-educated Englishman, accompanied by his attractive and obviously intelligent Chinese wife, was a different proposition. The

Chinese quickly came to understand that our company's assistance from London often made the difference between success and failure for them in evaluating and accessing the Western engineering technology that they were looking for.

The chief Chinese official of the Chinese trading company with whom we mainly worked was a seasoned negotiator and a good English speaker, from whom I learned much. Working in partnership on several deals, we became, if not friends, at least trusted colleagues. My key role was to work with the decision-makers of the European company involved, while he associated himself with the Chinese buyer. From time to time we would meet together to compare notes and discuss ways to solve problems which had arisen during negotiation. Our relationship became particularly important when the negotiations got stuck, which often happened over the amount of money which the foreign company was demanding, or the type and modernity of the technology which the Chinese buyer was permitted under the contract to acquire.

An example of this occurred when a Chinese company based in central China which made equipment for unloading ships became interested in conveyor equipment for grain and coal. The technique for moving large quantities of these commodities was known as 'en-masse' conveying. It depended on the characteristic of these kinds of commodities to stick together and behave like a solid if the conveyor equipment was constructed in the right way. This made it much easier to move large quantities. The

Chinese told me, via our Beijing office, that the company who had invented this technology and developed it in the 1920s and 1930s was British, and based near Bristol in the west of England. There were other companies who had similar technology, but the British company was the best, in their opinion, and was the one they wanted to acquire technology from. But their approaches from China to the company, by fax and by telephone, had met with silence. They estimated the value of the technology transfer at around one million dollars. I considered that a fee of ten per cent on this contract size would not make us rich, but would cover our costs with something over, at a time when we needed to build up a track record of success. I decided to undertake the business.

I contacted the British company, and spoke to their managing director. He was aware of the Chinese efforts to discuss a technology transfer with his company, but he had not responded to their approaches because his company wanted to keep their knowhow to themselves. He told me that they had received many approaches from Russia, America and elsewhere, but so far he had never agreed to sell their knowhow because it was proprietary. However, after visiting his factory and meeting with him and his senior executives, I persuaded him to consider doing this transaction and entertain the Chinese delegation, on the condition that the technology which they would sell was not exported or shared with any other companies inside or outside China.

A month or two later, the Chinese delegation arrived in London, and were transported by us to the West Country. I met them at the factory, with a member of my Beijing staff who was an experienced interpreter.

The negotiations started. Within a day or two, it became obvious that success was unlikely. The price expectations of the Chinese factory director, who was also the delegation leader, were far away from those of the British company, who felt strongly that the Chinese should be paying a lot more than they expected for a conveying technology which had few real global competitors. At one point, the British team left the negotiations and returned to their offices, claiming that there was no purpose in continuing the discussion, because the Chinese failed to recognise the true value of what they were trying to acquire.

The situation looked hopeless. I sat down with the Chinese negotiator to see if there was some way forward. Clearly, the Chinese had to improve their offer significantly. He agreed, and proposed that perhaps the British would be attracted by the opportunity to do a joint venture in China with the Chinese factory, which was very strong in the Chinese market. The combination of the British reputation and knowhow with the Chinese market strength could be a successful combination. Moreover, this idea might help to break the deadlock between the two sides. I said I would discuss this with the managing director of the British factory, and emphasised to my Chinese counterpart that there would be no basis for discussion unless the Chinese side came up with a significantly improved offer. On that note we parted, he to discuss further with his Chinese colleagues, and me with my British ones. Later I saw him sitting opposite the Chinese factory director and speaking forcefully to him. I didn't need a translator to understand that he was explaining that this was a golden opportunity for the Chinese, and that if the factory director did not take it, he would regret it for ever. The British side appreciated the gesture made by the Chinese, and said they would think about it; meanwhile, they said they were prepared to listen to a better offer, but it had to be significantly better.

When both sides met again the following day, tempers had cooled, and there seemed to be some possibility of progress. Nevertheless, I was surprised, and so were the British, when the Chinese doubled their price. Clearly, walking away from the transaction had been an effective move, because the Chinese side did see an enormous potential market for this conveying technology in China. Although the British side did accept this revised price in principle, which actually exceeded their expectations, and the negotiations moved onto the details of how to transfer the technology, they did not want to take up the Chinese offer of a joint venture. They explained that they were not a large enough company to justify the time and effort which it would take to make a joint venture project work. Selling their knowhow for a cash sum appealed to them, provided that the technology was restricted to the Chinese market, because they had recently completed a management buyout.

A focus on near-term revenue and profit, as against deciding on a longer term, riskier and more ambitious strategy which could bring far larger benefits eventually, was something that I saw time and again over the six or seven years that I spent advising British companies in China. This was true both in technology transfers, like the above transaction, or when I was assisting companies to enter and develop the Chinese market for their products and services. In this case, once the Chinese company had fully absorbed the conveying knowhow, from the engineering drawings and instruction which they were given by their British partners, they were in a position to extend their market leadership in the Chinese market. Today, that Chinese company is a dominant player in the Chinese ship-loading and conveying market. Just imagine what that could have meant for the British company who had the opportunity, nearly thirty years ago, to share this adventure.

British economists and politicians look enviously at Germany's exports to China, which amount to five times those of Britain, and they wonder how that is. Many think it must be because Germany has a weaker currency. This analysis displays a common misunderstanding about competitive advantage. Germany's industrial advantage in China lies in its long-term management perspective, and emphasis on quality and research. A machine which costs fifty per cent more but lasts three times longer and produces a better quality product more consistently may be more expensive to buy, but offers much better value. Volkswagen has become the world's largest car manufacturer because it invested in two Chinese joint ventures in 1983 to produce cars for the Chinese middle class. Today, it sells more than three million cars each year in China. By contrast, Britain's last mass car producer, Rover, was acquired by a Chinese car manufacturer in 2003 for almost nothing. Under Shanghainese (rather than British) ownership, Rover has become one of China's leading domestic car brands, Rewe. Could there be a better demonstration of Britain's tragic failure in an industry in which, decades earlier, the country had been a leader? My role as Chinese industrial intermediary sadly gave me plenty of examples of British lack of ambition, unwillingness to invest for the long-term and focus on profits today.

Another project that we were involved in, at about the same time, provided another echo of Britain's once mighty industrial prowess. As usual, a contact from our office in Beijing was the starting point. Two factories in China, one in the south and the other in the north, wanted to acquire an identical technology, to remove wastewater with pumps that were designed to operate submerged for many years on end. The obvious company in Britain to approach was a Scottish pump manufacturer who was a world leader in this industry. I called them, to discover that they had already been contacted from China by one of the companies. But as we had brought them a second customer in the same country for the same technology, and our assistance would be very helpful in bringing the projects to a successful conclusion, it seemed to make sense to combine the two projects into one, and for our company to be appointed as the project agent. That is what happened.

A few months later, a Chinese delegation from each factory arrived in Scotland to investigate the pump knowhow, and I travelled north to assist our Scottish client with the negotiations. The Chinese were shown the pump factory and several examples of the submersible pumps operating. However, they insisted on being shown the engineering drawings, to prove that the Scots did indeed possess the knowhow. As soon as the engineering drawings were partially unfolded, a Chinese engineer from one of the delegations noticed my family name, Chance, in the corner of each drawing. (Perhaps he thought that I had made them.) On investigation, it turned out that the submersible pumps had been invented in the 1930s for the purpose of pumping out lighthouses, by an old Birmingham firm who had become the world leader in the 1850s in lighthouse optic and building construction. , until they were acquired one hundred years later by their competitor, who had later sold the submersible pump knowhow to the Scottish firm. The lighthouse company was my family's company, a famous glass manufacturer based in West Bromwich, in which my father, and his father and grandfather had spent their working lives. This historic coincidence was not lost on the Chinese, and probably contributed materially to their readiness to accept the technology as genuine. The final contract negotiation took place in our Beijing office, over a period of two weeks — to give time, as the Scots put it, for the Chinese to enjoy themselves negotiating.

Not all of the negotiations we arranged between Chinese buyers and European sellers ended successfully, and sometimes we had to admit defeat. One such case involved a Chinese fishing company from an island near Shanghai, called Zhoushan. Fish forms an essential part of Chinese cuisine, and the demand for it from the large Chinese population was obviously considerable, and growing fast. Thirty years ago, the construction of modern ocean-going trawlers was beyond the capability of Chinese shipyards. So it was that our Shanghai office passed to us in London a demand from China for an ocean-going, European-made fishing trawler.

On investigation, it turned out that the cost of a good second-hand vessel of this type ran into several million dollars. But apparently the client had the necessary funds. We started by concluding a commercial arrangement between ourselves and the leading London-based shipping broker Clarkson — an extremely competent and professional organisation — who became our partner in this affair. A delegation from Zhoushan arrived in London. Someone from our office met the Chinese party at the airport and showed them to their hotel in west London. By now I had met numerous Chinese businessmen. I had found it possible to form trusting and effective relationships with many of them, often by finding we shared a sense of humour. This was important in surmounting the hard bargaining which formed part of a successful negotiation.

But when I met the delegation from Zhoushan at dinner that evening in London, I felt little warmth. My attempts at breaking the ice by cracking my usual jokes fell flat, as they looked at each other in surprise. The next day we travelled to the City, and sat in Clarkson's boardroom while the available options were set in front of the Chinese. They could obviously not see for themselves every possible vessel which was on the market, but they did manage a trip to see one in Amsterdam. After several days of discussion and negotiation, the choice had been narrowed down to one fishing trawler which was only two years old, had been made at a top yard in Germany, and had a range of best quality modern equipment. The price was about three million dollars, of which our share, to be received through the shipbroker, would be 1.5 per cent.

Finally, the moment arrived when the Chinese had to make their move. Once again we visited the shipbroker's office in the City of London, to be told that another buyer of the trawler had appeared. But the broker continued, as the Chinese had arrived first on the scene, they had the first option to acquire the vessel. The seller was prepared to give them until midnight that same day to take up their option to buy. After that time, the window would close for the Chinese, and the second buyer would be given his chance.

I knew that the Shanghainese had a reputation for being the most commercially aware and money-conscious people in China — and that, in a nation of entrepreneurs and businesspeople, is saying something. But I was not confident that the delegation trusted me enough to act in time. In the taxi back to their hotel in London's West End, the Chinese were silent. I left them in their hotel to talk amongst themselves and eat their supper. Returning to my office, I was told by my Chinese assistant that the leader was keen to make the acquisition, but was being persuaded by a colleague that the midnight deadline was a negotiating trick, to force the Chinese to terminate their negotiations and pay the price which the seller demanded.

After supper and an hour or two before the deadline, I returned, with my assistant, to the hotel which the Chinese were staying in. I explained to them that this was the decisive moment, that it was now, or never. Their leader looked at me, and said nothing. I could see that he had been persuaded by his colleague that he should wait until the following day, when he could beat the price down some more. In vain, I repeated my exhortations, driven in substantial part by the fee which we would receive if the Chinese agreed to buy the vessel. But all my pleadings were in vain. I left them, silent and with determined expressions on their faces, a few minutes before the decision hour of midnight.

The next day we received a call early in the morning from the Chinese. They said they wanted to go on negotiating the price for the ship. I told them that the deadline had expired, and the vessel was no longer available to them. They refused to believe this, so I called the shipbroker, who confirmed the bad news. This information was passed on. I was not a party to the subsequent Chinese discussions. They left the following day to the airport, to return to Shanghai. My Chinese assistant, who conveyed them to the airport, told me that the leader was so angry that my assistant thought that the leader's colleague, on whose advice he had wrongly relied, would be in serious trouble when he got home.

The trust built up between me and my opposite number in the Chinese trading company, which had enabled other difficult transactions, was absent in this particular case. The Chinese did not trust me or the shipbroker, the deal failed, and the delegation from the Zhoushan fishing company went home to China without their sea-going trawler.

Our technology transfer business really started to take off late in 1991, when our Shanghai office started sending a stream of detailed technology requests from different Chinese factories based around Shanghai for the processing and machining of automotive and other components. As the end-customer was often the German company Volkswagen, operating through its joint venture in Shanghai, the technology solution to the component machining requirements often lay in Germany, because the world leading German machine-tool industry has grown up around the world leading German car industry. I started travelling to southern Germany on a regular basis in order to find out more about the various German machine-tool companies which could meet this demand.

At this stage, our competitors as intermediaries were entirely based in Hong Kong or sometimes Taiwan. When it came to winning contracts, we had an advantage by being based in mainland China, and by employing local Chinese people, because the mainland Chinese did not trust or like the Chinese from Hong Kong, whom they tended to regard as traitors, who had run away from the mainland, when the going got tough, to follow the money. The Shanghainese, in particular, have no warm feelings for the Hong Kong Chinese. Our company, on the other hand, was locally based, it employed locals, and we knew many of the key local officials and factory heads in Shanghai.

China, although ethnically homogeneous, consists of hundreds or thousands of local cities, each with their own customs, traditions, and even languages. Each of these local identities can be traced back thousands of years, to the time when China was broken up into many different principalities, each of which was often at war with its neighbour. Machiavelli's Renaissance book of statecraft, *The Prince*, was aimed at the leading families of the warring principalities of northern Italy; similarly, the original version of *The Analects* of Confucius, which was used in modified forms to teach Chinese rulers from around 100 BC onwards, was written around 500 BC, following many years of experience by its author of advising different aristocratic and ruling families in north-east China. China remains, even today, a very localised country, although it has a strong centralised Government. Shanghai, in particular, thinks of itself as separate from, and better than, the rest of China.

Most of the German companies I met were family owned, and employed between two hundred and two thousand people. I was deeply impressed with their focus on technical excellence, their willingness to continually invest, and their business capabilities. I travelled all over central and southern Germany to find the leading machine-tool companies in each important machining process (boring, grinding, polishing, measuring and so on). Because we were usually first on the scene with our China story, and I was European, I was able to establish agreements with several excellent German family companies to represent them in China.

In just over three years we developed a long list of successful technology transfer transactions, among which the Shanghai-based auto industry was predominant. It seemed at one point that our Shanghai office was winning every deal it went in for. I was aware that the Chinese factory buyers would seek three or four equipment and technology transfer quotations from different companies, each of which offered a proven technology at a competitive price. The buyers would then choose between them. Success sometimes depended on price. At other times, the buyer preferred one technology over the others. Another important factor might be that the buyer felt comfortable with the supplier he chose because he felt sure of quality and reliability throughout and after the transaction.

However, there was another reason for our success. Starting in 1991, our offices in Beijing and Shanghai had made it known to us that the Chinese decision-makers in these transactions expected to be looked after financially in order to make a favourable decision. Raised in an environment of propriety, at first I refused to countenance the payment of bribes. It was explained to me by my Chinese wife and business partner, that I could hold on to my Western ethics, and lose, or I could do business the Asian way, and win. Our competitors, Chinese firms based in Hong Kong or Taiwan, had no such qualms. I checked to see if British law forbade bribery. It did not (until 2010, when Britain's Bribery Law was passed). And the companies which we worked with, whether British, Italian or German, seemed quite used to the practice of making side-payments to key decision makers. They even had an expression for it: 'local commission'.

The side-payment amounts to start with were two or three thousand dollars, tiny in relation to a deal size of hundreds of thousands, or millions of dollars. But within a year or two, the bribes or local commissions had ballooned to tens and even hundreds of thousands of dollars. I was aware of the practice, but tried to salve my guilty conscience by not becoming directly involved myself, and by telling myself that there was nothing in British law which forbade bribery. The side-payments, or bribes, were all handled by our client through our local Chinese office between our European client and the Chinese buyer. However, I was concerned. What was the attitude of the Chinese Government? Could I continue to turn a blind eye?

It turned out that what I was seeing was a small part of a wave of smuggling, bribery and official theft which had appeared in China as the economy started to grow again in the early 1990s. I heard stories of naval craft belonging to the Chinese Navy being used to smuggle items whose importation into China was either strictly controlled, like mobile telephone handsets, or which carried very high import duties, like cigarettes, alcohol and luxury cars. The commonest smuggling route was from Hong Kong and Macao into China; heroin, strictly banned in China, came from Myanmar, and agricultural products which carried high import tariffs were smuggled in across the Chinese border with Vietnam. In 1993 members of the Ningbo Government and the local manager of the Bank of China branch were arrested, tried in a Chinese court, and sentenced to death for stealing millions of dollars from the bank. When the head of China's foreign exchange bureau threw himself out of a window, it was rumoured that he had been co-operating with a gang to steal billions of dollars from China's treasury. Some people said that Asia had always been this way. I believed them.

But 1993 was our first year of profit, and in January 1994, our second daughter was born. We celebrated by moving from our cosy but small office in Westbourne Grove to a prestigious office block in Victoria, near

London's Hyde Park. With a list of successful transactions behind us, and a roster of well-known companies as our advisory clients, we were set on the road to success. But not everything was perfect. We were hardly on speaking terms with our investor, and my hopes of establishing a model of corporate success and quality were being undermined by the regular practice of bribery by our office in Shanghai.

Moreover, I had succumbed to severe sciatica. I had to spend hours each day lying on the floor in my office to relieve the agonising pain shooting from my lower back and down my right leg. Sometimes I was even compelled to take telephone calls and even meetings lying on my back. The first London doctor I consulted told me that on a scale of zero to ten (ten being the worst), my case measured around eight. He advised rest until my condition improved. I spent a week lying in bed, and felt a little better. But as soon as I started work, the condition worsened. I switched to a recommended back specialist in Harley Street, a famous and expensive address for private medical expertise. But that was no better. It took me one year, and four osteopaths, before a young female chiropractor told me that the solution to my acute problem was simply to take more exercise, and to spend less time sitting in an office, in a car or in an aeroplane seat. She added that less stress would help. I couldn't do a lot about the stress, but as soon as I started to go swimming regularly, the condition improved, and today, it hardly exists.

By mid-1994 we had two new children, a business with rising revenue and a profit, but we also had problems with no obvious solutions. On balance, I felt as if I was ahead. We had proved that making a profit doing business with China was possible. In fact, more than possible. We had carved out a new niche. Could I find solutions to our problems while we built the business?

IV

TRIUMPH AND TRAGEDY

The first notice I received that the outside world was taking notice of us was in 1991, about two months after we had concluded the new shareholder agreement with our investor. It was early one morning, I was sitting by myself in our office above a shop in Westbourne Grove in Kensington, London, when the phone rang. Deep in checking financial projections, I answered it.

"Is that Giles Chance?" I answered that it was. "My name is Philip Lyons and I'm a great admirer of yours," the voice at the other end of the telephone said. Taken aback, I asked the caller what he admired. "We're a large sugar trading company which is converting its business to financial services. China is one of the areas we're interested in. We've been looking at what you do, we think you've done a great job, and we want to buy your business."

Was this real? My immediate reaction was that this call was a practical joke. Perhaps one of my friends had persuaded someone to pull my leg. After all, we had only been properly in business for eighteen months. Was the small enterprise we had created so special? I explained that we had just taken on a new investor.

"Yes, we know that. We've done a lot of checking. Your new investor is the wrong person to back your business. We have much deeper pockets. Let me tell you what we have in mind. We want you to sell us all of your business, including the China offices, your people and your current book of business. You won't be able to stop working for ever, but we'll pay you enough to take a nice holiday for a month or two, with a bit over at the end. It's a great opportunity for you."

By now, I had started to believe the caller was serious. But the obstinate determination which had carried me thus far now became an obstacle. Already I could see our business had great potential. This call served to confirm it. We spoke for a further ten minutes or so, at the end of which I asked the caller if I could think it over. Irritated by my lack of reciprocity, he started instead to count from six down to zero, at the end of which, he told me, he was going to put the phone down. I have never responded well to pressure of this kind. He counted to zero, ended the call, and that was the end of our conversation. I went back to my calculations. A few minutes later I heard my assistant climbing the stairs.

The second surprise arrived about six months later. I was sitting in Newbury in the county of Berkshire, about eighty miles from London, in the headquarters of Vodafone, discussing the progress of our Shanghai project with the responsible board director. Suddenly he changed the subject. "There's something I want to ask you." I waited expectantly. "We've realised that the development of a healthy phone retail market is the key to our future. The mobile phone market for the United Kingdom is developing too slowly. Currently there are a total of about fifty thousand phone subscribers, split between two phone companies. We hold about sixty percent of the market. We think the total phone market in UK will be about twenty times larger, about a million phone subscribers, with our share around six hundred thousand. To get there," he went on, "we think that the market needs a specialised chain of mobile phone shops which can offer attractive retail phone packages, and drive mobile phone ownership into the mass market. We've found a young man who is already selling mobile phones, and we're thinking of forming a joint venture with him. We need entrepreneurs, people like you, to help us make this project a success. You have an excellent education, and we've been impressed by the way you've started your own business in China and brought us into what could be an exciting project. Whoever gets in on our retail project now will end up making a lot of money. Would you be interested in joining us?"

Once again, I was surprised. This time, though, I felt favourably inclined. As a company, I liked Vodafone. They were dynamic, forward-looking and well organised, characteristics which contrasted favourably with some of the other British companies I had met. Their people were sharp and friendly. I replied that I was flattered at his confidence and interest in me, but I was a small part of the way through establishing an enterprise, and needed to think carefully about his offer. He accepted my answer, asked me to consider carefully, talk to my wife, and let him know in a week or so.

Although I had my hands full every day of every week, I did find the time to consider his proposal. It was generous and exciting. My main concern was leaving the company we had started in the hands of my wife and our investor. He had already shown his true feelings about her in the plane from London to Glasgow. Could I trust him? I didn't think I could.

A week later, I found myself back in Newbury for another follow-up meeting on the Shanghai project. Had I thought about the offer? I was asked. Surely I would accept? When I declined, such was the surprise and indignation that I invoked that I was subjected to a long interrogation about my reasons. At the end of this, I admitted my real reason for wishing to stay where I was. My interlocutor's face turned grim. He said, "In that case, I won't ask you again. Consider the matter closed".

Today, Man Financial and Carphone Warehouse are both dominant players in their respective markets, respectively of hedge funds and mobile phone retail. In the space of a few months in 1991, I was given the opportunity to join both, on the ground floor. But I preferred to stay with my own dream. That's being an entrepreneur, I guess. What others see as risky and probably impossible, you see as a challenge which you believe can be overcome. Part of the fascination lies in finding out if your vision can be made into a reality. When you find out it can, the reward is huge. But then you look for the next dream. Success brings its own challenges.

A couple of years later, I was taken to lunch by a head-hunter. He wanted to ask me about acquiring a well-known and larger competitor. The founder of the business was getting old. The son was not very interested in taking on the business which his father had created. So the old man, who controlled the business, was thinking of selling. The head-hunter said he could get the money together to do the deal, and he knew how much the other company wanted. By then I had been searching, without much success, for a new investor for a year. The corruption problems in Shanghai were getting worse, and my back was still giving me problems. I was beginning to think that I was not a buyer, but a seller. I passed.

With the business doing well, I was able to take myself away somewhat from day-to-day management, to search for some way of providing our investor with an exit and replacing him with a new partner who could support us in our next stage of development. I started meeting with small, specialised firms of financial advisers. Sometimes these only consisted of one or two people, usually in their late forties or fifties, who had decades of experience working for a merchant bank or an accounting firm. These conversations were always interesting, and it was pleasant to be treated as an important client and taken to lunch in an expensive restaurant. However, they didn't lead anywhere.

Meanwhile, my wife was beginning to spend most of her time with our young family. I absorbed most of the responsibilities she had shouldered early on, which focused on managing the Chinese offices. After several years of operation, these had settled down, and we had all learned how to work together. Most days, I would come into my office to find two faxed messages, one from Beijing and the other from Shanghai, with reports of the previous day's significant activities and any new openings for business. In turn, I would compose a message before I left each evening which would be sent to China. Every week, my wife would send a message in Chinese which would receive replies in the same language. It may seem foolhardy to expect Chinese employees six thousand miles away to remain loyal and behave honestly over a multi-year period when it is obvious to them that their efforts are generating revenue, booked in London, amounting to hundreds of thousands or millions of dollars. Yet they were honest, and continued to work hard.

As our revenue grew, I started thinking about how we should share the rewards with the people who had helped generate them. After a lot of thought, I developed a bonus scheme. At our investor's suggestion. we set up an equity-sharing scheme whereby our Chinese managers could become shareholders as well. My wife was against this idea, because she said that the Chinese were happy to think of themselves as employees. Once they became owners, she said, then their attitude would change. They would start to think about their responsibilities, they would no longer consider themselves as employees, and problems could arise. I supported the investor in this matter, partly because he knew that we disliked him (my wife refused to speak to him), and I wanted to make him feel that he was not excluded, at least until we found a replacement for him.

We went ahead with the employee share scheme, but found that my wife had been correct. Once we shared information about the business, instead of being even more supportive, as we had hoped, we found our China managers more demanding, and in some way, a little hostile. Our Beijing office manager considered himself, with justification, to be the senior manager as a result of his experience and the importance of Beijing in China. But when he saw from the accounts that the revenues from Shanghai had in recent years outstripped those from Beijing, he became jealous of his Shanghai colleague, and co-operation between them suffered.

Worse followed. I was becoming more concerned about the corruption with which our Shanghai office seemed to be getting more deeply involved. In the spring of 1994 I arranged a trip to Europe for our two China office managers, in order to discuss our strategy, and to visit companies in Britain, Germany and Italy whom we represented in China. The two-week trip was also intended to be something of a reward in the form of a holiday, with some sightseeing in Europe. The trip started in London, with some day trips north, south and west to visit British clients. Then we spent a couple of days in Stuttgart, a major automotive base in Germany, and visited several of our German clients. We then crossed the Alps to Milan. After another visit to an Italian client, we drove to Venice where we spent two days sightseeing, before returning to London.

Throughout the ten-day trip, our Shanghai representative carried a small suitcase which he never allowed out of his sight. He had announced earlier that instead of returning directly to China from London, he would be visiting New York for a few days, as he had relations who lived there. I suspected that the unstated, real purpose behind his visit to the United States was to deposit a large amount of hundred-dollar bills in a New York bank account. The money probably belonged to a number of the Chinese in Shanghai who had conspired to arrange transactions by Chinese factories of Western, mostly German technology for manufacturing auto parts. In those unregulated days of twenty-five years ago, taking large amounts in cash from corrupt jurisdictions and depositing it in developed country banks halfway across the world was a common and straightforward matter. Our Shanghai office manager had been aggressive in developing revenue. As a consequence (we later discovered), he had been targeted by a Shanghai-based ring of Communist Party officials and factory executives who needed a reliable link with foreign technology sources in order to realise their ambitions for self-enrichment.

How long, I asked myself, could this go on before the Chinese authorities found out what was going on? I was not worried that we in London would be caught up in a Chinese investigation. Although our Shanghai office was controlled from London, we had been careful not to become involved, ourselves, in the paying of bribes by our clients to win business. The 'local commission' was arranged by our Shanghai office to be paid to a local Chinese bank account by the company who signed the contract with the Chinese factory. It was a small proportion, usually one per cent or less, of the money which the European company received. But in a multi-million dollar contract, the bribe could still reach a large amount.

Another issue concerned the correctness of this conduct. I had been raised in a traditional English Christian household, where bribery in business was considered wrong, immoral, even despicable. So here I was involving myself in something I knew was wrong. I appeared to have fallen into a classic trap by allowing the prospect of financial gain to affect my moral compass.

In a short three years, our company had become prominent in the arrangement of technology and equipment transfers from European automotive suppliers to Shanghai. As a consequence, we were receiving unsolicited approaches from companies that we had never heard of, asking for our assistance in China. Obviously they had heard about our success. But I knew that the reason for our spectacular success in Shanghai (or part of it) was not only non-sustainable, but wrong. Could I find a way to terminate the role we were playing in Chinese corruption without destroying our company? I found myself in an awkward dilemma: on the one hand, a successful business and a young family, on the other, participation in corruption which, if not illegal in Britain (at least, at that time), ran counter to the moral principles I had been taught.

In the middle was our investor. I knew that since he had met our Beijing manager's secretary, he had stayed in regular contact with her. After I had rejected his demand to bring her to work in our London office, he had worked out another way to bring her to where he was. In early 1994, she resigned from our company, and arrived in Britain to study English at a language school in Oxford. I sensed that, although our investor had to be pleased at our commercial success in turning a profit, our business had become a means to his primary goal, which was to bring his Chinese girlfriend to a place where he could see her on a regular basis.

The strain of trying to keep several balls in the air simultaneously was beginning to affect me. We moved to the country, to live in a house with a beautiful garden which I thought my young children would enjoy growing up in. The problem in Shanghai came to a head a week or two later. Following our strong financial performance, we had paid a large cash bonus to our Shanghai manager Frank, which I had agreed to pay over a period of three months. He sent me an overnight email which objected to the delay, demanded the payment immediately, and referred ominously to people he knew who could help him to receive what he thought he was owed. For me, this clarified the position about which I had been fretting for many months. Clearly, Frank's financial success, combined with his new friends in high places in Shanghai, had changed his view of us and of himself. He had started to believe that the company depended on him, and therefore he could say or do whatever he wanted.

I thought carefully about this. Frank's contribution had been a significant factor in turning the company's financial performance into profit. For that I was grateful. I also recognised that he could go on generating even more revenue in the future. But at what cost? On the other hand, we now had a strong relationship with a number of European industrial, particularly automotive component companies, and a reputation in the fast-growing market for technology amongst Chinese companies in Shanghai, Beijing and around China. Overall, I judged that we could now manage without Frank, provided we could find a suitable replacement for him quite quickly. And most importantly, if Frank left, we could start again on a new platform and with a clean sheet as far as bribery was concerned. Of course, there was the possibility, even the likelihood that without the oil of bribery, securing deals in Shanghai could become more difficult. And we would have to find a way to deal with possible fallout from the people in Shanghai, in the mayor's office and elsewhere, with whom Frank worked. On balance, though my mind was clear. I had to terminate Frank's employment.

How to do this? I felt that matters in Shanghai had come to a critical point, and that speed was of the essence. I could speak to Frank over the phone, and send a message by facsimile immediately to the other people who worked in the office to inform them of the new situation. Frank would hand over his office files and then leave and they would be expected to stay until a new manager could be found. In the interim, I would appoint the senior engineer who worked for us as the temporary manager. I knew the Shanghai personnel quite well, having met them on several occasions, and having communicated with them frequently by facsimile and telephone. We paid them well, and I felt sure that this fact, plus their loyalty to my Chinese wife, and to a lesser extent, to myself would be enough to prevent them leaving. This proved to be the case.

The next morning I called Frank and told him the bad news. I asked him to hand over the work files and the bank account and to leave the company by the end of the week, once the handover had been completed. He protested, but I told him that his previous message had overstepped the line, and we had reached a point of no return. I thanked him and told him my mind was made up.

Looking back now, I think that the months of worrying about the corruption issue, together with trying to conceal my growing dislike of our investor impacted on my decision- making abilities. My bank manager, who was continuing to be extremely supportive, told me at a meeting shortly afterwards that I was looking exhausted and he was worried about my general health.

However, matters did not improve. Following the dismissal of Frank, we held an emergency board meeting, at which it was decided that someone had to travel immediately to Shanghai, stabilise the situation and recruit a new manager for our office. We turned to the only board member who spoke Chinese, and that was my wife. She had recovered from giving birth ten months previously, and we had a full-time nanny who lived with us to help look after the children. The problem seemed manageable, although I would have to spend some of my time supervising the nanny, and looking after the children when she took her days off over the weekend. We expected that my wife might have to be away for no more than a month.

In the event, my wife was away for nearly four months, and our nanny handed in her notice after Christmas. I could not blame her for leaving, because she had helped out over several weekends and even spent part of Christmas Day with us. When she left, I became the child-carer while I looked for her replacement. I quickly discovered the true realities of the British childcare market. After spending several days with nanny job search agencies, with one small child balanced on either knee, I managed to recruit a girl who could join us the next day. With the children in the back of the car, I drove thirty miles to a railway station to meet her. Once we got back home, I felt much better. Within an hour, though, the telephone rang. It was from the nanny search agency, for her. Another job had come up, in Dubai, and she wanted to take that. Obviously, it was better paid. In vain I protested that she had just arrived. That same evening, I had to drive her back to the railway station. We were alone again.

Eventually I managed to find several local ladies who could come to the house for a few hours each day, to look after the children, while I rushed to the office in London.

My wife had arrived in Shanghai, and had met with Frank and the rest of the office staff. She thought she had found a replacement. The situation seemed under control. But she sent me a message by facsimile to tell me something she could not say over the phone: that she was being followed, her hotel and office telephones were both bugged, and she had received a telephone call in the hotel room the night after she arrived from someone calling themselves a friend, who offered to drive her around the city.

I knew that the people who were behind the corruption in Shanghai would be worried when Frank left our company. However, I believed that Frank would explain to them who we were, and that we wished them no harm. I did not expect them to threaten or attack my wife, and in fact, they did not. Still, the situation was highly unpleasant, and I spent many evenings lying awake in bed wondering what was happening on the other side of the world. Frank's replacement was a capable woman, in her mid-thirties, who had worked in the Chinese hotel business, spoke English quite well and seemed to be unflappable. Most importantly, this woman was a close friend of my wife's family, and my wife felt she was completely trustworthy. We decided to offer her the job, and to our relief, she accepted immediately.

Having stabilised the situation in our office, my wife turned to trying to unravel the corruption business — who was involved, and what was their feeling towards us. For this, she had to travel to Beijing to visit another family friend, a retired minister, who had the high-level government connections necessary to make detailed enquiries. It turned out eventually that at the heart of the Shanghai corruption business was a branch of the Chinese military intelligence based in Nanjing. They were effectively above any kind of law, were independent of the police in Shanghai, and were sufficiently powerful to be able to co-ordinate a number of factory heads and key Shanghai Government officials in a complex scheme of bribery involving many factories in the Shanghai area who were acquiring technology and machinery from overseas.

It was the individuals from the military intelligence office in Nanjing who had contacted my wife when she arrived in Shanghai. While my wife was in Beijing, we assumed that her telephone was not being listened to. We discussed at length if we should take any action. I was against bringing the matter to the attention of the police or the government in China, where corruption was a crime punishable either by a prison sentence, or in very serious cases, by execution. There was no guarantee that the officials to whom we reported were any less corrupt themselves, and they might decide that we were as guilty as the Chinese. My wife agreed, we let the matter rest, and she returned to London a couple of days later.

A month or so later, our investor announced that he was resigning as a director from the company, although he would continue as a shareholder. He gave as his reason that he thought that Frank's dismissal as Shanghai manager had severely impaired our business, and he did not want to be involved in a failing business because it might impact on his other business activities. A feeling had been growing inside me for more than a year that our business had become less important to him. His resignation confirmed what I already suspected: that by acquiring a Chinese mistress he had achieved his main aim. Probably, I thought, his wife, who knew about his arrangement with his Chinese lover now based in Oxford, had drawn a line and told him to cut his relationship with us. I told him that our business continued to be satisfactory, and on present trends we were likely to record another annual profit. But he did not change his mind, and I accepted his resignation.

A weight had been lifted from my shoulders by our investor's announcement, and we felt free, although he remained the majority shareholder until we could find a way for him to exit the company. My new sense of freedom was short-lived. A month or two later, he informed me that he wanted to sell our business to a trading company in London which had interests in China, and wished to expand their small advisory business by adding ours. I understood that his wife had given him the choice of divorce, or parting with his China connection. But I thought that, perhaps, this could offer a solution to our board problems. It seemed a good fit. But my wife and I did not want to lose our independence, to merge with a competitor whom we had bested on several occasions. Our potential partner had had several very profitable years with their commodity trading business, but their advisory business was weak. That's why they saw our business as a good fit for them.

At the time of the merger negotiation in mid-1995, we were involved in a large contract to sell a special machine for manufacturing truck wheels to a factory near Shanghai. Our industrial, manufacturing partner in this business was an American company located near San Francisco. Ying had to join the Chinese delegation in San Francisco to assist in the contract negotiations. I conducted our business merger negotiations in London without her. Our investor appeared at the table beside me in his capacity as owner of fifty-one per cent of our business. At a meeting beforehand, he informed me that he had discussed a deal in outline with the other side, and the terms appeared satisfactory to him.

But the other side had done their homework well. They focused on the essential weaknesses in our position: that Ying and I were at odds with our investor, that we were tired, and we had two small children. Although we had had one profitable year, and would shortly record another, the other side homed in on the weakness of our balance sheet after three years of start-up losses. They announced that they were prepared to merge the two businesses together, but they were not prepared to pay anything for the equity of our business. They informed our investor that he would receive nothing from them, and he could leave the meeting. They were interested only in the original founders, and wished to talk separately with them to conclude an arrangement.

Two emotions conflicted in my mind. I realised that the other side had worked out a way to get our business for much less than its intrinsic value, but when our investor began to protest, and was rudely cut off by the other side, I said nothing. After a long pause he stood up, and left the room.

I was left alone with the other side, who became much friendlier. While they proposed paying nothing to our investor, they suggested that they appreciated our efforts and success, and we would be compensated by them for completing this transaction. Our business would be merged with theirs, and we would join their company as directors. The cost savings from merging our offices in London and China with their offices approached half a million dollars annually, an amount which would obviously pass straight into profit, assuming that revenue could be maintained. They needed our co-operation in order to persuade our existing clients to bring their contracts, revenue and goodwill across to the new merged business.

I countered that the transaction they proposed could be considered to be unlawful, because the three shareholders in our company would receive unequal treatment. Ying and I would receive financial compensation, plus service contracts as directors with their company, but our investor would receive nothing. The reply was that we were being treated not as shareholders, but as valuable future employees who needed some incentive to support their proposed transaction.

It was an ingenious concept, and I could not help admiring them for the way they had attracted our investor and led him on, to persuade him (and then us) of the future benefits of the merger, only to discard him at the moment of truth. I told the other side that I would let them know my response by noon the following day. They agreed to this.

The other founder, my wife, was still in San Francisco, where she was fully engaged with looking after the six-man Chinese delegation and their negotiations. We stood to earn a fee from a successful transaction in San Francisco of more than fifty thousand dollars, so it was important that she should stay on the west coast and see the business through. The investor had left the picture. I had to make the decision on my own, and I had only a few hours to make it. I believed that our business had the momentum and the track record to make it without a merger with anyone. Our investor's money would stay in our business as he had no way of extracting it. After initiating the process to sell our business, his interest had changed, and he would now be strongly in favour of rejecting the merger proposal and continuing to trade as an independent business.

But the recent turn of events and my wife's prolonged absences since going to Shanghai the year before had drained my energy. Our children were three years old and eighteen months old. I felt strongly that they needed a stable home, above all the presence of their mother, instead of a succession of nannies, with their father looking after them at the weekend. My wife was due to return in a week or two. But how long would it be before she had to leave again, to return to China?

After six years, reaching profit, and with a diverse client base, the business prospects for continuing were good. But I felt the cost to my family was too high. I decided to accept the merger proposal. Giving up our independence and abandoning the upside of equity ownership was a bitter pill to swallow, but I felt reassured that the proposal would allow my family to settle down, in particular, for my wife to stay at home with our children. After a long transatlantic call with my wife, I informed our merger partners that I accepted their proposal. We commenced the merger process.

The next month was a painful one, as the edifice of reputation and good faith which we had built up as a business was demolished by the business merger. It was moving for me to observe and feel the loyalty from our staff in China when I visited them to close our Beijing and Shanghai offices. Even our bank manager in London, who had assisted us as we built up the business, expressed his regret. He told me that he thought that his bank would have supported us until we could find another investor. The shared vision and passion which had brought us success became strangely clearer as it faded. Our client contracts and revenue could be transferred to the new corporate entity, but not our corporate spirit and identity. While the merger process ran its course, and indeed afterwards, I kept reminding myself that this way was better for my family and that was the most important thing.

Should I have rejected the merger proposal and persevered as an independent business? Although the founders — myself and Ying — were compensated by the new business, the amounts involved didn't at all match the upside of equity ownership which we abandoned. I wondered many times whether I had been over-protective of my family, and if I should have continued. But the emotional and physical demands on us had become very great, and I feared for the future of our children if we were both fully engaged in the business during their early years. The course I took reflected my own values. Looking back more than twenty years later, and given how things turned out later, I don't regret it.

V

STARTING AGAIN

The next few months were the most difficult I had ever had to deal with. Ying returned from successfully doing a deal in California to find that our business now belonged to someone else, and we had lost all the money we had invested in it. We were salaried employees, and had given up all the equity in the business we had created from scratch. The outcome was bitter for both of us. However, Ying could now spend her time at home with our two young children, concentrating just on motherhood. I was busy with joining our business to our new partners, but still had plenty of time to reflect on whether it had been right to give up so much, in return for relative security and certainty. But when I thought of our young children and remembered the months when Ying had been away in China, I felt I had made the correct decision, painful though it was.

I had slipped up badly, but I believed that, still in my mid-forties, I could recover. The experience I had gained, of starting a business, of China and of myself, was all invaluable. I still saw China's rise as inevitable, but I was in a small minority. Most people doubted China's ability to overcome its enormous challenges of size and of backwardness, while the country remained in the grip of a largely unenlightened, centralised system. In 1995, China as a modern successful country seemed to be an unrealistic vision as much as it had in 1989.

But I had seen and heard the Chinese at first hand, in ways few foreigners had. I had travelled widely in China and had been part of their first steps into the outside world. I knew how determined, clever and united they were, and I knew that they thought their time had come. Mao's revolution had damaged China, but it left behind a sense of unity, while China's size and long history gave them their self-confidence. The consequence of six years close-up was that I believed even more in China's future.

For me, others' doubts were not a hindrance but a help, in that they gave optimists like me much more room to work in. Imagine if everyone had believed that China was the place to be for the next fifty years. We would all be trying to get through the same small door at the same time. I concluded that once I had placed myself and my family on a sounder footing, I could start to think again how to achieve the dream I had started with, of building a business around China's ascent.

After spending two months finalising our business sale transaction, closing our offices, and moving myself to our partner's office in another part of London, I said goodbye to my family and transferred myself to China, to fulfil my agreement to spend the next year there merging the two businesses into one. While my wife lived at home in England with our children, I based myself in Shanghai, and took a room in the city's most famous (but not most expensive) hotel, the Jin Jiang, located in the centre of the city on Mao Ming Road, opposite the beautiful old French embassy, which was then (as it is today) a Japanese hotel. Mao had stayed in the Jin Jiang Hotel when he visited Shanghai after the war, and my wife's parents had held their wedding reception there in 1950. The décor was pre-war, but so was the service, and the Chinese food was the best in Shanghai.

From there, I could see Shanghai being rebuilt. Huaihai Road, the Bond Street, Park Avenue or Faubourg Saint-Honoré of Shanghai, joined Mao Ming Road a few hundred yards from my hotel, and a subway station was being constructed at the junction. Opposite was a cinema, and around it stood shops selling buns, cakes and the Shanghainese version of the French croissant, because my hotel stood in what had been the French part of pre-war Shanghai. The Shanghainese had become very attached to French baked products, and in fact made lighter and tastier pastry than can be found anywhere.

It was rumoured in the mid-1990s that one-third of the world's high-rise cranes were located in Shanghai. It certainly seemed like it. Driving from my hotel to the Shanghai airport at Hongqiao, a distance of about ten miles, could take three hours or more, as the car stopped and started from one long queue to the next. The city was building the overhead inner ring road, a construction which required huge supporting pillars to be built every few yards. This entailed emptying and knocking down rows of pre-war colonial houses, each of which accommodated several Chinese families. Shanghai in the mid-1990s was a forerunner of every Chinese city. The reconstruction which started in Shanghai then still continues around the country, and has become the largest building boom the world has ever seen, in the process producing the world's largest steel, cement and construction companies.

With the assistance of Western investment bankers in Hong Kong, the city of Shanghai was the first in China to develop a money-raising corporate structure which caught the imagination of global investors. China's huge potential has always had the capacity to awe and to thrill. When the country's economy started to recover in the early 1990s from the shock of Tienanmen Square, the braver kinds of Western investors, including some large European and American multinationals, started to believe once more that they could see opportunity in China.

In 1994, Shanghai tapped this optimism, by wrapping up several government owned businesses in a corporate vehicle called Shanghai Industrial Holdings. New shares in Shanghai Industrial were sold, via an initial public offering on the Hong Kong stock market, to the international investment community. The sale of an ownership stake of about thirty-five per cent to the investing public raised the hundreds of millions of dollars which the city needed to develop its infrastructure, starting with the elevated ring road round the city centre, referred to earlier. Other foreign sales of shares in government controlled companies which owned assets in Shanghai raised more capital to fund the development of the Pudong area, which lay on the southern, largely unused side of the Huangpu river, an arm of the mighty Yangtse which flowed through the centre of Shanghai and gave the city its name as the Dragon Head of the Yangtse river basin.

Once again the Shanghainese had shown themselves to be the most farsighted, capitalistic and enterprising people in China; this was the reason why Chinese leader Deng Xiaoping had overcome conservative resistance to removing Shanghai's leash in 1992. Shanghai's money-raising schemes were quickly followed by other cities, starting with Beijing, which was wise (or lucky) enough to float its own municipal money-raising vehicle in August 1997, just when the tidal wave of bullish stock market sentiment peaked, before crashing spectacularly as the Asian crisis bit hard. Beijing Enterprises raised its money from the public at $65 Hong Kong per share; a year later, the share price stood at around $12.

In the mid-1990s, the community of foreigners living in Shanghai was beginning to grow fast. Multinationals were starting to send promising middle-ranking managers to live there, often as a testing ground and a prelude to fast internal promotion. Modern hotels like the Portman and the Ritz-Carlton had appeared, incorporating modern accommodation blocks. Single foreigners lived in those, or if they were married, in newly built housing developments near the airport. I was considered by my expatriate colleagues to be somewhat eccentric, as a foreigner at that time in Shanghai, to live in a Chinese hotel. But the consequence of this choice was that I saw a lot more of the Chinese side of Shanghai than most of my expatriate contemporaries, which provided insight into the underlying dynamism and capability of the Shanghainese. It underlined my earlier confidence in China's potential as a major commercial power. I started to turn over in my mind how I could use my experience to start another business in China.

Meanwhile, I was kept fairly busy integrating our own operations with those of our new partner, which required frequent travel between Hong Kong, Shanghai and Beijing, whose development lagged that of Shanghai. It was as if Shanghai felt they needed to show their northern controllers where the real ideas, wealth and dynamism lay in China. As for Hong Kong, it was nearing the end of a long boom which had started in the early 1980s, mirroring China's emergence. Travelling between Shanghai and Hong Kong was a heady experience, with both cities growing exponentially, and the B747 planes which carried me on Air China between the three cities were always full.

Because I saw China's huge commercial promise in the longer term, I continued encouraging British companies to get involved in China. One of the most interesting visitors I had was the chairman of a famous British pharmaceutical and convenience store company. He had been honoured earlier in his career by British

Prime Minister Margaret Thatcher for his leadership of British military procurement, and subsequently had been raised to the peerage. I was able to arrange an interesting programme for him which stated with a tour of Puxi, the old part of Shanghai, and continued with a reception given by the Shanghai Government in his honour. Here he spent half an hour in conversation with a vice mayor of Shanghai. In fluent English, the Chinese vice mayor outlined the city's detailed and long-term development plans, explaining that they were designed to return Shanghai to what its people considered as their rightful place as the most important city in east Asia. The plans included new high-rise blocks which would house up to ten million people. These new suburbs, he explained, would need convenience stores and pharmacies. He invited my British guest to set up a chain of stores in partnership with the Shanghai Government.

Sadly, the response was lukewarm. My visitor had been alarmed by the number of idle building sites and cranes in Pudong, which he interpreted as a sign of an imminent Chinese crash. He preferred to invest in Thailand, leaving China to braver spirits. I saw this as another missed opportunity for British industry to get in on the ground floor in China.

After a year, I felt that my handover task had been completed. Although I was encouraged to engage in the new business, my heart lay elsewhere. Ying was now a full-time mother, so my worries about the children had dissipated, but I wanted to spend some time with them before they went to school and grew up. I also wanted to work out how to take advantage of what I had learned. I resigned, to return home to Britain, and consider the next step.

I had left a message at home to say I was on the way back, but when I arrived back home on a beautiful spring morning at our house in the English countryside, the family were all asleep, and both front and back doors were firmly locked. The first person to hear me was my eldest daughter, who appeared briefly in the kitchen in her pyjamas before disappearing upstairs to wake her mother. It was a joyful reunion; it had not been easy for my Chinese wife to survive on her own in the English countryside with two small children.

After a few months working part-time in London to help an Asia-focused hedge fund to expand its understanding of Chinese markets, I accepted an offer to work as a China specialist from a new investment bank which had a focus on emerging markets. The job required us to relocate to Beijing and to establish a branch office there. This fitted in with my personal ambition to give my children some early experience of China, to start learning Chinese and meet Chinese children, while I would be able to spend time with them every day. My wife's father was a well-established professor at one of the leading Chinese universities in Beijing. His wife, my mother-in-law, had followed the traditional Chinese custom by spending six months with us in London when our first child was born, so she had got to know our household well. But her husband did not know us at all. I saw this period as important for our family to become properly familiar.

We found accommodation in Beijing close to my father-in-law's university in the north-west of the city, where the children would attend the kindergarten and primary school which belonged to the university, and which provided excellent and greatly sought after education. Our apartment opposite the university front gate was in a ground floor apartment block behind a hotel. We shared a communal private garden. It was a ten-minute walk to the children's school, even closer than that to my wife's parents and close also to the shops.

Our bank's regional office was in Hong Kong. I was in Beijing because it was the best place to get beneath the skin of Chinese Government policy and to meet senior Chinese politicians and businesspeople. By 1996, the Chinese airline system had developed to the point that every large city had an airport, and it was now possible to fly all over China from Beijing, to visit companies and regions. I could transmit the understanding I gained via written reports and telephone conversations, to the bank's clients around the world. I missed the excitement and fulfilment of running our own business, but I enjoyed the interest, the relative lack of stress and the very generous salary.

Beijing was very different to Shanghai. The city, originally a regional capital, had been built in the 1200s and 1300s as the headquarters for the Mongol Yuan dynasty. The Emperor's Palace had been added in the

1400s by the conquerors of the Yuan, the Meng dynasty. On a clear winter day, one could see the hills which ran away to the north, from which the Manchu who occupied Beijing in the 1600s had come. The palace, which had housed twenty-four Chinese emperors, was carefully positioned to lie north-south at Beijing's centre, and the Chinese Government's principal buildings lay close by. The city's north-south axis still followed that of the Emperor's Palace. A huge picture of Mao hung (and still hangs) at the entrance to the palace, overlooking the huge square called 'The Gate of Heaven' or Tienanmen. It was a statement that new management had moved in after the hundreds of years of imperial occupation, but in a sense, Beijing was unchanged. Its friendly people knew they were inhabitants of the city at China's heart. They were not traders like the Shanghainese, and they had no need to look over their shoulders to see if the government approved of them. If anything, it was the other way round: the Chinese Government has always been very sensitive to the feelings of the Beijing people, because that is where the government officials and leaders live.

When we moved to Beijing at the beginning of 1997, the city still lay largely within the outer, or third ring road, which passed close to our apartment. From where we lived, villages, countryside and fields, with hills behind were still visible to the north. In central Beijing, there were still only two subway lines, both of which had been built in the 1950s and '60s. One of these followed the line of the old Beijing city wall which Mao Tse-Tung had had demolished during the cultural revolution as a symbol of old, unreformed China (against the protests of a history professor from Peking University, jailed and tortured for his trouble). The other followed the major central thoroughfare, Jianguomen, as it ran east-west past the Forbidden City and Tienanmen Square. Beijing citizens were still poor, and most lived in government accommodation, where they paid a small rent. For ordinary people, noisy buses spewing noxious exhaust fumes provided the main way of commuting. At that time, ownership of home dwellings by private individuals in China was still unknown. Most food was purchased in markets. The principal modern department store was the one which we had been involved in establishing in 1991, in the Lufthansa Center in the west of the city centre. There, for a high price, one could buy a wide range of modern Western clothes and accessories, with imported Western food in the basement. Another modern store had just opened, a few yards from our apartment in the northwest of the city, because the area around the university was designated to be a major high-tech zone. Today, this area is the centre of a start-up zone that rivals California's Silicon Valley in geographical and financial size.

Most vehicles, including cars, were still owned by companies, not individuals. A common sight on the Beijing ring road was the large blue three-tonne trucks made by the car factory Dongfeng ('East Wind') in central China, belching black smoke from their diesel exhausts. These trucks were often to be seen by the side of the road, heavily overloaded and broken down, waiting for a mechanic to get them going again. It was a far cry from today, where China's huge vehicle market, by far the largest in the world, generates Chinese-made vehicles whose design and performance equals any other country's.

Traffic accidents caused by Chinese drivers who had only just passed their driving test, or had never taken driving lessons, were frequent and often violent. The most spectacular that I recall was when a motorbike carrying two people was struck at speed on a Beijing ring road crossover by a large truck travelling fast in the opposite direction. One of the riders was thrown high up into the air before he fell to the ground. There was no doubt that both the people riding the bike had been killed. The bike itself was turned in the blink of an eye into a tangled, squashed mass of metal.

The Beijing climate was continental: sub-zero winters, with blue skies and snow, and forty-degree Celsius summers, with hot dusty winds. A fortnight of spring and autumn separated the two main seasons. The Beijing people loved their city when it was windy and they could fly kites, or when it was cold, and they could wrap up, throw snowballs, visit the beautiful Winter Palace which with ice, snow and its poetic, leaning willow trees looked like a Chinese painting, and eat hotpot. Numerous factories dating from Mao's industrialisation still operated all over Beijing, including highly polluting steel and chemical plants. The canal inside the city was black with effluent. But the air pollution had not yet become the choking fog that it was to become fifteen years later. Blue skies in winter were still the norm then in northern China, especially when the east wind blew and the temperature dropped below zero.

Beijing was still a city of small communities which had not yet been obliterated by the massive concrete and glass buildings of today. Most of the large buildings, like the Great Hall of the People, the various ministries, research centres, large enterprises and the army barracks in the centre of Beijing had been built on massive Russian lines during Mao's regime. The reminders of China's imperial past were few: only the Forbidden City in the centre, the country palaces on the northwest outskirts, and some remnants of the old wall still remained. Near to where we lived, one such palace, which had belonged to an uncle of the emperor, housed Peking University. It contained a marble boat on a lake, in imitation of the marble boat constructed in the summer palace in the 1880s by the Empress Cixi using the funds given to her by the Western powers to construct a modern navy which could defeat the Japanese and hold the balance of power in east Asia. Its aristocratic builder paid with his life for having the impertinence to imitate the imperial design. There were a couple of relics of the great Beijing city wall, including the massive Drum Tower, which the Red Guards had omitted to knock down. The hotel to which our apartment belonged was a joint venture between overseas Chinese and the Chinese Army, who were deeply involved in commercial affairs in China (until the army was formally banned from involvement in commercial activities in 1998). Our front gate was guarded by youthful Chinese soldiers, who would often play with our children as they ran around in the garden outside. We were part of a community, and felt it.

Across the road, the children attended kindergarten and primary school in the People's University. They were able to get places at these excellent and exclusive schools because my father-in-law was a well-established and famous professor at the university. The rules for entering this exclusive primary school were very strict. Only children of university academics could attend the school for free. Otherwise, parents had to pay a large sum of money. Our children did not qualify for free education. But my mother-in-law had been a biology teacher at Peking University high school, and had taught the headmaster of the primary school when he was a child. She was able to use the teacher-student relationship, which in China is sacred, to get much reduced educational fee terms for her grandchildren. Without those family links, we would have had to pay a lot of money, even in those relatively un-monied days in China, to get places — if we could have applied. Then and now, good Chinese schools in China fail to meet the demand from the education-mad Chinese, and those with good reputations are oversubscribed to an extent that makes getting into Eton, Oxford, Choate, Yale or Harvard look simple. In China, personal relationships mean everything.

The first deep restructuring of China's economy, under Prime Minister Zhu Rongji, had started a couple of years earlier, throwing off an estimated fifty million middle-aged unemployed from state-owned companies. These individuals had signed up, after they left school in their late teens to the local state-owned company, to spend their lives performing often meaningless tasks in an enterprise which produced poor-quality products which no one wanted to buy, but were often forced to buy through lack of alternatives. We employed one of these unemployed unfortunates as a cook in our home in Beijing. She had worked as an internal accountant in a state-owned company in central China. Now, out of work in her fifties, with no transferable training or career future, she was staying with her son in Beijing. He was an acquaintance of my wife's family, so we found her a job. We wanted to help, but she couldn't cook at all. After two months working for us, she left tearfully, with three months' advance salary in her pocket.

My job was fascinating, and I enjoyed working with a new bank which focused on 'emerging countries' in Europe, Latin America and Asia. In the mid-nineties, China was still perceived as a dragon which was very much still asleep, and it was barely on the edge of the radar screens of most investors. But living there and visiting Chinese companies all over China, as I did, one could see, in fact, that the dragon had awoken.

Private ownership had not yet become formally accepted by the Chinese Government. But by asking questions and walking around, it was easy to see that almost all of China's productive economic activity was private in nature. The usual way for this to occur was for a local Chinese entrepreneur, or group of entrepreneurs, to combine with officials from the local government to found and develop an enterprise. The Chinese service sector was primitive, and when they thought of work and the economy, most Chinese then thought of factories. Today's multinational Chinese computer, smartphone and server company Lenovo started as a company called Legend in 1984 in Beijing, as a joint venture between some enterprising computer scientists and an important government owned body called the Chinese Academy of Social Sciences. In a country like China, where the state oversees everything, the participation of a government entity was vital for success. Government officials could get the operating licences and capital from the local state owned bank for the business to kick off, while the local entrepreneurs supplied the ideas and the drive. Often the local government would make life hard for outsiders, either Chinese or foreign, who competed with enterprises in which the local government were sponsors. There were many ways in which the local government could do this. For example, they had the power to ban competing products on grounds of safety or non-conformance. Or they could delay the provision of essential utilities, like power and water.

The government sponsored private companies registered their holding organisations offshore. The British

Virgin Islands in the Caribbean was a popular legal jurisdiction for these informal commercial associations between Chinese Government officials and private businessmen. The British colony had tax advantages, as well as strict rules about shareholder privacy which made it impossible for an outsider to discover who the ultimate beneficial owners of an enterprise actually were. At this time, these enterprises always focused on manufacturing, and usually got going by copying some Western product which was widely used in China, like a computer, a modem, a foodstuff or even a car, and then selling it with a Chinese label at a fraction of the Western price. Computers, foodstuffs and modems are relatively simple to copy and manufacture. But Chinese vehicles or aircraft based on copies of Western originals didn't work so well, because making a car or an aeroplane requires mastery of a wide range of technologies which are complicated, expensive to acquire, and difficult to coordinate. But in any industrial process which required large numbers of people working in an extremely disciplined way, like textiles or simple machinery, Chinese companies were already making an impression. It was thus, multiplied millions of times throughout the huge country, that the determination, hard work, inventiveness and risk-taking of the Chinese became the critical success factor in the Chinese economic miracle.

My hand-picked colleagues at the investment bank, based in Hong Kong, New York and London, were talented and stimulating. After my years a decade earlier managing large sums of money in London, it was interesting to be positioned on the other side of the business, between Chinese companies who needed risk capital, and Western institutions who were looking to invest it. I realised that China was already attracting a lot of funding from the developed world, and would attract more. That was only one part of the growing relationship of mutual benefit which was starting to tie China to the rest of the globe. But one factor set China apart from other emerging countries. Its people saved a large proportion of their incomes. Financial prudence was part of their culture; but moreover, they were fearful of their future in a country without a social safety net, in which most people could remember the Cultural Revolution. As time went on, the large and growing pool of Chinese savings would not only finance most of China's own needs, but would also be lent out to other countries who needed finance, especially the United States, whose people generally lacked the saving habit. Financial markets were going to be an essential part of the China development story. I started to think that I should look in that direction for my next enterprise.

In its suddenness and ferocity, the Asian financial crisis, which burst upon the global economic scene in 1997, was like the credit crisis of ten years later in the West. The cause, though, was different. South-Eastern Asian countries had done very well in the 1980s and 1990s by making inexpensive goods with cheap, plentiful labour and selling them to developed Western countries. America became a key market for these countries, and it made sense for the Asian producers to lock their currencies to the American dollar, so that the value in dollar terms of their growing exports did not fluctuate. As these countries grew, Asian exporters sucked in debt to finance expenditure, much of which was in American dollars. Their economies heated up and price inflation increased. Rising inflation placed downward pressure on the value of local Asian currencies against the mighty dollar. Governments from Thailand to Indonesia resisted this downward pressure on their currencies, because they knew that a lower domestic currency would increase the value of the dollars which they as governments, and many of their companies had borrowed, making their foreign debt payments harder to meet. Western hedge funds based in New York and London noticed the debt repayment mismatch and started to attack one country after another, selling their currencies and buying dollars. The battle between each Asian country's dollar reserves and the hedge funds only lasted for a couple of months before the country's dollar reserves ran out, and the hedge funds won, collected their large winnings, and moved on to the next vulnerable Asian country.

The result of these foreign raids was chaos in the target country's financial markets, as currency collapse was quickly followed by mass bankruptcies, when dollar debt became unrepayable. The finances and economies of Thailand, South Korea and Indonesia disintegrated, unemployment soared, and social unrest forced the collapse of one regime after another. A picture sped around the world of the head of the International Monetary Fund forcing the Indonesian dictator Suharto to step down, in return for the financial support from the Fund which the country desperately needed. Malaysia only survived by enacting draconian regulations which locked essential capital inside the country and kept out the pirates from Wall Street. Singapore and Hong Kong, with their sophisticated capital markets and large pools of dollar reserves, seemed safe. The agrarian economies of Vietnam, Laos and Cambodia were simply too undeveloped to be much affected by the crisis.

This Asian financial storm started a few months after our arrival in Beijing. As it worked its way around the region, starting with Thailand and moving onto to Malaysia, South Korea and Indonesia, we in China wondered how and when it would hit us. At that time, most of China's economy was still closed to the outside world, and much was still agrarian. This made it possible to think that we in China could remain unaffected. But in Hong Kong, things were warming up as capital, which hates uncertainty and turmoil, started to leave the former British colony in search of safer havens. (Hong Kong ceased to become a British colony, and formally became part of China in October 1997 under the 'one country, two systems' rubric.)

As foreign investors fled for the safety of New York and London, our bank started to close offices. In April 1998, I was standing on the floor of a mini-tractor factory in the canal town of Changzhou, near Shanghai, when I received a call on my mobile phone from New York. Our outpost in Beijing was next on the list for closure. It was disappointing because we had been hoping that we could hang on until the worst of the storm had passed. The month before, we had opened a smart new office in the World Trade Centre in central Beijing. I think the building's management were more surprised than anyone when I informed them of the cancellation of our lease.

Meanwhile, our family was happy and settled in Beijing and our children liked their school, so we decided to stay and tough it out. With every financial institution withdrawing from Asia, it was hard to find new employment. But our generous contract termination terms gave us some breathing space. Ying took a part-time job advising a large British power company in Beijing which was trying to unravel several one-sided and uneconomic Chinese joint ventures brokered on its behalf in the early 1990s by an unscrupulous Hong Kong intermediary. I was recruited by a friend to advise a small brokerage based in Hong Kong and London on a part-time basis. This kept me in the game, while providing plenty of spare time and allowing me to continue developing my own ideas. The expatriate community in Beijing had built up strongly during the boom years of the mid-1990s. Most large multinationals now had a Beijing office, and some of these housed dozens of staff.

The major international media were also well represented. We met many China correspondents, and some became good friends. One, a Harvard-educated Australian called Peter, headed Bloomberg's Beijing office and had a large off-road 4x4 vehicle which enabled exploration on the empty hill-roads outside Beijing. With Peter and his soon to be wife Yin, a Chinese archaeologist from Peking University, we spent many weekends walking in hilly, wooded countryside to the north of Beijing while we discussed Chinese politics, in particular his pet obsession with what really happened to Mao's Long March General Lin Biao, controversially killed with his wife and family in an aircraft crash in Mongolia in 1970.

The next China episode in my life started when one day, my journalist friend Peter called me from his office, to tell me about a Chinese internet celebrity whom he had recently interviewed in Beijing for Bloomberg. The man's name was Edward Zeng, he had just appeared on the front cover of *Time* magazine and he had become famous because he had set up the first internet cafés in China. I learned that Edward was a graduate from China's MIT, Tsinghua University, who had spent time in Canada, and returned to China several years earlier with a vision. Peter suggested I should meet him to learn more, and gave me a mobile contact.

Intrigued, I called the number. The phone was answered in a deep North American voice with Chinese intonation. I introduced myself as a friend of Peter, the Bloomberg journalist, and said I was interested to find out more about the internet cafés. We arranged to meet. I didn't realise then that this was the beginning of my extensive relationship with China's digital industry, today the world's largest.

VI

BEIJING, ME AND THE DOTCOM BOOM

I visited Edward Zeng the following day. He had taken over part of the Capital Stadium building, a huge Russian-style monstrosity which has survived Beijing's architectural makeover, and still stands on Beijing's second ring road, about twenty minutes by car from where we were then living. I remembered visiting the stadium in 1988, when I first came to Beijing, to watch a Chinese pop concert. It must have been the only public space in Beijing then large enough to hold many thousands of people. (The Great Hall of the People was huge, but strictly reserved for official Communist Party and state functions. A Chinese pop concert certainly did not qualify.) Even in the late 1990s, good quality modern office accommodation in Beijing was scarce, and what existed was expensive. I had got used to visiting the Beijing headquarters of multinationals and large Chinese state owned companies in offices converted from Chinese Government guesthouses.

A building near the Capital Stadium gate, which had served previously as a guardroom or external kitchen, had been converted into an internet café. I poked my head inside. It was packed, with every seat taken, and more people standing in line to take their turn. The clientele were all Chinese of student age, and mostly male. They were glued to their computer screens, reading news or sending messages to their friends on one of the Chinese language websites which had sprung up in the last year or two. I withdrew my head, entered the main building, and was directed to Mr Zeng's office by one of the young English speaking Chinese I found inside.

Edward Zeng, the youthful boss, sat behind a large walnut desk. His office contained a sofa and several large armchairs. He stood and introduced himself. He was of medium height, powerfully built, with piercing brown eyes and a commanding presence. He moved gracefully to an armchair, and motioned me to sit in another. Ignoring my introductory civilities, he started to explain his background and his vision. After graduating from Tsinghua University in Beijing, he had emigrated to Canada to seek opportunities. There, he had made money by introducing Chinese companies to list their shares on the Toronto Stock Exchange. While he was in Canada, he had seen companies like Amazon and eBay start their business in the United States, and this had given him the idea to become China's first internet tycoon. He had returned to China in 1996, had founded China's first internet café, and now, three years later, he wanted to develop China's first e-commerce site. His company was called Sparkice, because he would use the internet and his entrepreneurial skill to 'bring fire and heat to the frozen Chinese economy'

Edward told me that he believed the world was on the edge of a new era, in which the internet would become the medium for every kind of human interaction. China lacked a modern retail industry, but at the same time he knew that Chinese consumers, once they had money to spend, would become the most powerful economic force in the world. He saw the potential applications of internet-based commercial activity, which he described as e-commerce, as a huge future opportunity. Sparkice would be the first company to exploit the internet in China to develop trade between companies, between consumers and companies, and even between consumers. He described these three areas as B to B, B to C and C to C. I inferred that the B stood for business and the C stood for consumer. He asked me about my background, and said he was looking for someone like me, with a knowledge of China and experience in banking, to help him raise money from private investors to realise his vision.

All this took only a few minutes. It was impossible not to be impressed by Edward's grasp of his subject, the thrust of his dynamic personality and the force of his ideas. I bought some time to absorb what he had said, by asking him how an entrepreneur like he had managed to overcome China's notoriously tough and exclusive rules which limited foreign or private involvement in internet (or 'value-added') services. He replied that his company had a joint venture with Unicom, one of China's two state companies which had a licence to operate telecom and internet services. (The other was China Telecom, which had resisted any encroachment on their monopoly until overridden by China's forceful and competition-encouraging Prime Minister Zhu Rongji.) Edward's joint venture with Unicom had been awarded a licence by the Chinese Government to operate internet services. He considered that to be a vital way to keep other competitors, particularly foreign competitors, out. The important thing, he went on, was to be the first into this market, and then build fast, to get scale. He had already raised one or two million dollars from private investors. Would I invest? If not, he needed a detailed business plan which he could place in front of investors and institutions. Could I help him to write one?

I had already used email, I had read about the American start-ups Amazon, America Online and eBay, and I could grasp the essence of Edward's argument. I knew that the Asian economic crisis had presented a restructuring China with a huge growth problem. China's student population was growing fast, thanks to the baby boom of the 1970s. Every year, about seven or eight million young Chinese left school or college and needed a job. Many of the government owned companies who would have provided cradle to grave employment before the restructuring did not exist any more. The Chinese Government had turned to their export industry to solve the problem. They needed fast export growth to create employment and fill the growth gap left by the thousands of Chinese state companies who had hit the wall. If eBay in America could arrange auctions over the internet, then, I imagined, why couldn't the same internet be used to link overseas buyers in Europe and America with Chinese factories? The whole export process, from discovery to initial contact, arranging samples and order placement, even payment, could be internet-enabled. At least, in theory. By providing the software, marketing to the Chinese suppliers, and managing the process, Edward's company could act as the intermediary. Sparkice would only need to charge a fraction of each transaction to make itself extremely wealthy. I suggested this approach to Edward.

He replied that in his mind was another possibility, of selling products to Chinese consumers over the internet. I agreed that this was potentially a huge opportunity, but it lacked several essential links. Almost all Chinese were still poor, many did not have bank accounts, and none had bank cards. There were no internet payment systems in China, and the means to deliver large quantities of ordered goods to buyers did not exist. Some of the same shortcomings applied to my idea of using the internet to facilitate international trade, but even the introduction of buyer to seller would be a useful service which buyers would pay for.

Edward agreed that this might be a good way forward at this early stage of the internet's evolution in China. After some bargaining, we came to an agreement that I should write a business plan for Sparkice and should take my fee in shares in his company. He rose, took me down the corridor, and we entered another office where I was introduced to Jordan, a young Canadian lawyer who would draft our business agreement. While we were discussing the contract and the work, another person walked into the room. His name was Muhamed. He had met Edward at a conference in the United States. Muhamed was a Pakistan-born engineer who had graduated from the California Institute of Technology on America's west coast. He had recently made a few million dollars when the internet payment start-up which he had joined (Verifone) went public in the United States. Now he was reinvesting some of his winnings in Edward's Chinese project. I was introduced by Edward to Muhamed as the 'new member of the team', who would be writing the business plan and helping out as chief financial officer. I was taken aback by my sudden promotion, but didn't object. I realised that Edward had already gathered a few qualified people around him. Two hours after arriving at Edward's office, a stranger with a sense of curiosity, I left as a member of the Sparkice team. In the world of the dotcom boom, this was the new normal.

Edward was certainly an inspiring individual, and on the way back from our meeting to join my family for supper in our Beijing apartment, I was already turning over in my mind how I could present a vision which was compelling, and yet realistic enough to persuade investors to part with large amounts of cash for a project with no revenue and not much of an organisation.

Writing business plans and constructing spreadsheets was something I had learned to do, ad nauseam, while at business school in the United States. The mechanics of the process were almost subconscious. I had all the boxes ready to fill. What would I put into them?

Once back home, I tried explaining to my wife what had happened. But I found it was impossible to convey the sense of excitement and adventure which the meeting with Edward had created. When she asked me how many people worked in his organisation, and how many clients they had, I realised that perhaps I had been taken in by a confidence trickster, and it was all a fraud. But I persevered, and a few days later I had produced a fifty-page document which set out the vision which Edward and I had discussed. I hoped that the pages of financial projections which I had generated would make up for some large gaps in other parts of the document, particularly in execution. How would the software work? Who would make it? Was the Chinese internet fast enough to enable foreigners to communicate smoothly with Chinese companies? How would the payment system work? And so on. To make the financial projections look interesting, I had assumed that business revenue would start to grow in a few months, and would pick up quickly to a point where Sparkice could show an operating profit within three years.

In April 1999, I presented the plan to Edward, and we sat in his office while he called in the others to have a look.

I was expecting to have to spend a lot of time explaining the gaps in my plan and justifying the fast upward curve in revenue which appeared in my financial projections. Not a bit of it. Edward was delighted to have something which looked credible.

It was then I realised that the dotcom craze had reached China. Over the course of the next few weeks, the trickle of international investors and investment bankers visiting Sparkice in the Capital Stadium turned into a flood. They were all looking for the same thing — a project which could be listed within a few months on the stock market. Our timing, for the purposes of raising money, was perfect. Everyone was caught up in a frenzy of speculation. I remember that at one meeting we had with a leading American investment bank, in May or June 1999, we were told that, to sell Sparkice shares to the public on the stock exchange, all we needed to show was one quarter — three months — of sales revenue.

What these investors and banks wanted was something they could believe in, and the dotcom boom was encouraging them to believe in a lot. Edward was in his element. He had a vision, and it was a really good one, honed by many discussions with industry experts, other visionaries like him, and bankers. He knew all the buttons to press. It wasn't long before a queue had started to form to put money into Sparkice. First was Masayoshi Sun's financing vehicle Softbank, already famous for making billions in Japan from investments in the Japanese telephone company Docomo. In 1998, Softbank set up a subsidiary in China which looked for dotcom investments, and in the spring of 1999, they invested in Sparkice. A month or two later, they found another internet startup in China, called Alibaba which had just been set up in May 1999 by a former Chinese tour guide and English teacher called Jack Ma, and they invested in that too. In fact, Softbank invested in all four of the leading Chinese internet start-ups, and then sat back to see which would work out. I was intrigued to see about ten years later, when Alibaba appeared as a listed company on the Hong Kong stock exchange, that the main focus of their business model, then, was on using the internet to market Chinese manufacturers to buyers based overseas. I wondered where the former English teacher in Hangzhou had got that idea from.

The Softbank investment was followed by another, from a German whom I shall call Werner Gauch. Werner was an aerospace specialist who had made enough money from introducing Airbus to the Chinese in 1992 to be able to retire from the German aircraft company Dornier, and buy a large house on a lake near Basle in Switzerland, from where he ran his investment business, much of which focused on the country where he had made his first millions, China. I don't know where Edward met Werner Gauch, but by midsummer of 1999, they had agreed a plan whereby Werner would himself invest in Sparkice and would also introduce major German retailers, like Metro and REWE, as strategic investors alongside. Werner did things the German way — thoroughly. I realised that the whole business was getting serious when we were visited by a due diligence team from one of the Big Four accounting firms, because I knew that the cost of hiring four or five accounting professionals for a month ran into the hundreds of thousands of dollars.

I particularly remember that, among the many other visitors who arrived at the Sparkice office in the Capital Stadium, was the chief executive of NASDAQ, the technology-based stock exchange in New York. He had arrived the previous night from New York to persuade China's second telecoms operator, Unicom, to list its shares on his stock exchange. His meeting with Unicom in central Beijing was scheduled at ten a.m., the day following his arrival. His Chinese organisers had calculated that it would take ninety minutes to drive from his hotel to Unicom's office. Unfortunately, they miscalculated. The Beijing traffic that day was so bad that it took them over three hours to travel about a mile and a half, and the NASDAQ party's arrival at Unicom clashed with the sacred Chinese lunchtime hour of noon. The meeting was cancelled, probably because Unicom, a Chinese state-owned company, never had any intention of venturing as far as New York for its public listing. When the NASDAQ CEO arrived to meet with us after lunch, his Chinese delegation of organisers looked still to be in shock following an American eruption over lunch. Edward was a brilliant presenter, however, and the NASDAQ CEO recovered some of his balance and good humour as he was led by Edward into the brave, new, non-existent world of Chinese e-commerce.

Sparkice was formed as a joint venture with China Unicom. Edward saw this as the jewel in his crown because foreign-owned enterprises (which Sparkice was, with its company registration in the Cayman Islands) were prohibited by Chinese law from operating telecoms value-added services on Chinese soil.

This law remains in place today. Mention of it finds its way every year into the annual accounts of some of the largest companies in the world: Alibaba, Tencent and the other Chinese internet companies listed on public markets in Hong Kong and the United States. The legal device used to circumvent the regulation is based on the usage developed by Sparkice and the other pioneering internet companies of the late 1990s. It is a so-called back-to-back arrangement, whereby a Chinese national who owns the Chinese operating licences agrees to transfer the revenues from the Chinese licences to an offshore vehicle, from where the same revenues are transferred again to the listed vehicle in which the public invests. Instead of outlawing this blatant attempt to circumvent the regulations, or changing the regulations, the Chinese Government uses the back-to-back rule as a way of controlling the Chinese social media and e-commerce companies, some of which (like Alibaba and Tencent) have become enormously powerful and influential within Chinese society, by implicitly threatening them with the possibility of being closed down for breaking Chinese law. Such are the subtle ways in which the Chinese state controls private enterprise.

America's dotcom boom continued to strengthen, with its high priestess Mary Meeker of the American investment bank Morgan Stanley cheering it on. These were the times when, if you got it, you were cool, and if you didn't, you would be left behind, to be acquired by somebody much smarter who wore jeans and a T-shirt, or just left to die on the rubbish tip of history. Stock prices of companies with any kind of technology content or potential soared, leaving relatively pedestrian but solid companies in their wake. In this heady environment, company leaders previously known for their staidness and caution suddenly emerged as high rollers. The cash machine known as Hong Kong Telecom was bought by a young Hong Kong entrepreneur from the ancient British colonial relic Cable and Wireless, in return for new stock certificates in the entrepreneur's company of wildly inflated value. The British company General Electric Corporation, once the largest company listed on the London stock exchange and no relation of America's GEC, sold off its dull, uninspiring, but profitable collection of electrical engineering businesses which its newly retired founder had spent his lifetime acquiring, changed its name, invested in dotcommery, and quietly sank beneath the waves. The king of email, America Online, used its stratospherically high share valuation to merge on an equal basis with the largest American media company, Time

Warner. AOL's founder Steve Case had read his history books, and was smart enough to know when to check out.

The dotcom wave arrived in China early in 1999, and Sparkice surfed it. In a few short months, the company progressed from a ramshackle collection of young, expatriate and Chinese individuals working in a graduate school environment in a broken-down old building in Beijing on a speculative plan which might work in a few years, to an acknowledged leader in China's brand new internet industry, with financial backing of twenty million dollars. Edward Zeng was the main reason why. His vision was inspiring, and looking back twenty years later, remarkably accurate. Like Jeff Bezos of Amazon, Edward was a visionary. He saw how e-commerce would emerge from the internet, and he was able to explain his vision clearly and persuasively.

Edward participated at the beginning of a new cultural wave which he also foresaw: the emergence of China's high-tech entrepreneurs, a class of business people who saw huge opportunity in China's emerging economy, who wanted to merge Western training and technology with Chinese style and values to create a new kind of private Chinese technology company. I believe that the characteristics I saw in Edward are common to many of this wave of Chinese entrepreneurs who, we can now see, are affecting and will affect the pattern and speed of global progress. I will describe them. Edward was ambitious, hard-working and highly intelligent, with a high sense of self-worth and a strong will, qualities which together drew people to him. His values were Chinese, not Western. He was an acute observer of people, with their strengths and weaknesses, a quality which enabled him to develop relationships and use people to his advantage. His main weakness was his pride, and I think eventually his success made him overconfident, to the point that to an extent, he thought he could manipulate people who were senior executives in large organisations, and much more experienced than himself, to behave in ways which were foreign to them but which suited his purpose. I think he also lacked the integrity to lead an organisation, without which it is impossible to gain and hold the trust which, ultimately, employees, shareholders and other stakeholders depend on. In short, he was a formidably competent and persuasive, but flawed individual.

There was nothing in Edward's background which had given him experience of managing a high growth enterprise or a group of talented people. Edward knew this. He was aware that he had to develop a style and capability as a manager. Unfortunately, in his desire to incorporate Chinese values into his company, Edward chose, as his management model, Chinese communist leader Mao Tse Tung's style of 'divide and rule'. This meant that he would move from one member of his team to another, turning the full power of his personality on, and then, just as quickly, turning it off. This was a highly effective technique to use on his Chinese team members, but didn't work so well on the foreigners, who were more sceptical of using personal magnetism as the overriding management technique. He also suffered from another important weakness, one common to many independently minded risk-takers who strike out on their own. He could not take a back seat or give important tasks to other people which might give them the opportunity to stand out or look as if they controlled the company. Although Sparkice, with its newly acquired cash pile, impressive board members and promise of riches, was able to lure experienced English speaking Chinese executives in their late thirties and early forties as employees, Edward could not make the necessary style change, from cheerleading and inspiring a small group of enthusiasts to managing a complex talent group several times larger.

Through the summer months of 1999, I was part of Edward's core team. There were about ten of us. Some were expatriates like Jordan, the Canadian lawyer, his friend Peter from the University of Toronto law school, and Muhamed, the investor from California who had had personal experience of a successful high-tech startup. Most of the others were Chinese, some educated overseas, who focused on the issues of technology, helped to manage the key relationship with the Chinese Government joint venture partner Unicom, and marketed to Chinese exporting clients.

Edward kept everything close to his chest, so that we all had to depend on him for information and direction. I found that being involved at a senior level with one of the first Chinese tech start-ups was highly significant. From knowing nothing about the internet and its applications, within a few short weeks I became an 'expert' in a world in which a little knowledge gave a lot of power and influence. Second, I observed at first hand the workings of a Chinese company. As Sparkice grew rapidly from ten to one hundred people, Edward's relationship with everyone in the company remained a vital factor. It was his vision and personality which dominated the company and glued its various parts together. This patriarchal, highly personal style is certainly a characteristic of Chinese companies, even the new high-tech ones. It distinguishes them from Western companies and I believe it's a permanent feature of Chinese companies. Jack Ma at Alibaba, the e-commerce company, is (or was) a good example; Ma 'Pony' Huateng at Tencent, the Hong Kong listed social media company, is another.

As the company grew, I observed the problems which Edward faced in changing his style. The successful fund-raising effort and the attractive dot-com strategy had brought a number of experienced executives and bankers to the company's board. I believed that this combined experience and weight at the top of the company would help Edward to locate a leadership approach which was better adapted to Sparkice's increasing complexity and size. I was much more concerned about his other key weakness, of undercutting people who he thought might be threatening his control of the business and its direction. Hanging onto their 'baby' is a common phenomenon amongst business founders. If the growth is very fast, as Sparkice's was in 1999 and 2000, then this weakness is accentuated. Having seen Edward isolate members of his team on several occasions, and having experienced the treatment myself, I wondered if this was a flaw which would prove terminal.

As I found myself being drawn ever deeper into Sparkice's fascinating business and exciting possibilities, my wife informed me that the time had arrived for our children to return to Britain for schooling. We had discussed several times the possibility of educating our children partly or entirely in China. In those days of twenty-plus years ago, this would have meant going through the Chinese educational system. At the primary level, with which we had so far been involved, the Chinese system was excellent. It focused on learning by rote, which for young children provides a very good way to acquire basic literacy and numeracy skills. My elder daughter could recite her twelve-times table at the age of seven, in Chinese. But this rote-learning approach to education persisted right up to the end of secondary school, because at age eighteen every Chinese student would sit the three-day Chinese college entrance exam, known in Chinese as the 'gaokao'. This exam determined whether a student would attend a Chinese college, and if so, which one. In a closed system like the Chinese one, it was a person's passport to life, because good jobs in China's government or state owned sector were only offered to students from a small group of elite Chinese universities. My wife was convinced that the British model of education, with its emphasis on free and independent thought, was much to be preferred to the Chinese one. We discussed it some more, then decided to put the decision on hold while we went on a four-week diversion — a journey to western China and Tibet.

The trip was special, because we were able to go with a couple of very experienced Himalaya hands, plus another hanger-on with a good line in quietly humorous and telling comments, who (we found out at ten thousand feet) was also a goodish bridge player. Our three comrades-in-arms were in their late fifties and mid-sixties, but unlike us, they had a lot of Himalayan walking experience. Coming respectively from Bangkok, Beijing and London, we met up in Kunming, a pretty south-western Chinese city close to Myanmar (known previously as Burma), Vietnam and Laos, and notorious as the centre of the Chinese drug trade since pre-1949 opium days. In China, drug trafficking is punishable by a bullet in the head (the Chinese believe that the prospect of a bullet does focus the mind of criminality), but this does not deter the really hard cases. And there are no harder cases anywhere than amongst the Chinese criminal fraternity. Kunming is also the Chinese production centre for the legal narcotic, tobacco, and with its altitude and year-round temperate climate hovering around 25 degrees Celsius, boasts of many other flowers and plants. Nominally we were following in the footsteps of Forrest and the other great Victorian plant-hunters who had populated English gardens with the magnificent rhododendrons and other flowering trees of western China and the Himalayas. But Ying and I were very curious to see for ourselves what the eastern Himalayas looked like, and the kind of people we would find living there.

After a profitable visit to the Kunming botanical garden and a temple or two, we took the half-day car journey by car to picturesque and still unspoilt Lijiang, the original Shangri-La, and then climbed, again by car, into the foothills of the Himalayas to Deqin on the border of China and Tibet, stopping occasionally to inspect carpets of yellow primulas and admire the view, on roads which seemed only to climb, from one peak to the next. Rounding a turn with a rockface on one side and a plunging precipice on the other, we missed colliding with an oncoming SUV vehicle by inches, ending up with our vehicle teetering on the brink of a precipice which plunged to a fast-flowing river far below. After having a chat, and in my case, a smoke with the Chinese policemen who occupied the oncoming vehicle, we got back in, our minds focused, to complete our journey.

In Deqin we stayed in a hotel not unlike a Buddhist monastery, and met our trip organiser, an unusual British man of middle age, who had married a Tibetan and had adopted Tibetan nationality. He introduced us to our route and our guides. Our tour would feature as its central point a sacred mountain Khawa Karpo , which could be seen distantly from our Deqin hotel. The trip, which would take us about three weeks to cover, described a large circle which included two peaks of around fifteen thousand feet, several valleys as low as three thousand, and the crossing of two rivers which lower down in their courses would become the Mekong and Irrawaddy. Even up in the mountains, we were to see that both were hundreds of yards wide and fast-flowing. After taking possession of a highly accurate trekking map showing distances and heights, which had been made a year or two previously by a Japanese team who had covered the route, we met our guides. The team consisted of seventeen mules and seven Tibetans acting as guides, cooks and mule-handlers. We peered at the Tibetans, and they at us, and I don't know who was the more inquisitive and curious about the other. Meanwhile, the mules flicked their ears and tails at us, thinking of us, I suppose, as their new source of torment. The Tibetans ranged in age from eighteen to about thirty. They laughed and smiled a lot, and were fond of dancing to Tibetan music, which they would often indulge in when we stopped for the night and had finished eating.

After a night of heavy rain, we started the next day, only to find after a few hundred yards that the road was covered, anti-climactically, with a mudslide. This took several hours to clear, and by the time we set out on foot across the narrow rope bridge across the river dividing China from Tibet, it was well into the afternoon. We adjusted our plan, climbing a few hundred feet to a village where we decided to stop for the night. Near to the Chinese border, we found the Tibetan villages to be reasonably prosperous, with televisions, small general stores, motorbikes and even the occasional 4x4 which could travel over the rocky, half-made tracks which served as roads.

After a week of travelling, we found villages of a different kind, with no TV sets or bikes, where the mothers brought us their sick children and asked us for food, which we gave them. Clearly, the Chinese influence and control over the villages near the border did not extend further inland. Reality struck on the second day. Our lungs heaved as we toiled ever upward toward the pass called Dong Sha-La which crossed the mountain chain dividing China from Tibet. I wasn't fit at that early stage of the trek, and I don't ever remember a more demanding day of walking, with stops every few yards to recover breath. Our Tibetan guides rushed up and down the mountain urging us on, and the mules, which climbed the steep paths at a fast walk, soon disappeared over a ridge line above us. We attempted to persuade the Tibetans, some of whom spoke Chinese, that we were acclimatising, but I don't think they fully appreciated our difficulties. We staggered on in a line, each one of us bent, counting every step before the next rest-stop.

At ten thousand feet, the thick vegetation of rhododendrons and conifers, some enormously tall, gave way to a grassy moonscape, on which occasional blooms of brightly coloured flowers — white, yellow, red and blue — stood out. Eventually, in late afternoon, exhausted, we reached a meadow where we camped beside a rushing stream from which we could see the pass soaring above us. It took us another day and a half of steady, exhausting climbing before we crested the mighty peak, and started gratefully to descend.

A day later, we found ourselves down in a valley, staying in another village. And then we climbed again. We started to acclimatise, we started to talk to each other en route, and the trip became less a battle for survival and more a fascinating expedition of epic scale and once in a lifetime strangeness. As pheasants rocketed from bushes beside our path, I envied them their long shallow glide which took them over valleys several thousands of feet deep to another ridge a mile or two distant. Sitting and smoking a cigarette, I realised that the Himalayas were far larger in scale than any other mountains I had ever seen, or imagined, with drops of five thousand feet and more between ridgeline and valley floor.

One of the steepest and scariest drops we navigated was when our path approached the Tsambo river, which became the Mekong when it entered Vietnam. Rising deep inside Tibet, it had already become a huge river hundreds of yards wide, with a tremendous flow of water and a current in which no mule or human could expect to survive for very long. We followed our guides with the heavily laden mules as they picked their way along a winding path cut into the steep rockface which plunged hundreds of feet straight down to the river. At one point where our path rounded a buttress in the rockface, it narrowed to the width of a man's shoulders. Grimly looking ahead of us, not down at the cascading river, we wriggled our way past. I was astonished that the mules, with their heavy loads of tents, cooking equipment and food had managed to pass this narrow point. But they had, without a murmur. I remembered that mule trains had played a vital role in the jungle expeditions of the Chindits in the mountainous country of Burma during the Second World War, carrying heavy ammunition, food supplies and gun-parts up and down steep jungle paths, and I had read how attached the mule-drivers had become to these sure-footed animals, with their remarkable stamina and individual, obstinate characters.

Our mules went very well for two weeks and then, deprived of proper grass on which to feed, started to lose their energy, and had to be driven along for the last part of the trip by the mule-drivers belabouring their private parts with sticks.

After ten days, we split our party, with the two dedicated plant-hunters following a wider circle, and the three remaining (including my wife and myself) turning east to head back, in stages, to our starting point at Deqin, because Ying and I had to return to Beijing where our children were being looked after by our Chinese nanny and my mother-in-law, and Sparkice needed my urgent attention.

A few days later, we found ourselves on a grassy Tibetan hillside next to an old schoolhouse outside which stood huge walnut trees covered with fruit, with a river running below us. We made this into a base where we rested for several days, before attempting the last great climb back over the highest pass of all, which we had to cross in order to return to our starting point. There was plenty of grass here for the mules, but we had used up most of our supplies of food, although we still had tea and sugar. Our Tibetans visited the nearest village where they acquired a goat, some chickens, eggs and a few vegetables. These kept us and them going while we rested and conserved our strength for the final stage. We had all lost twenty or thirty pounds in weight, but we felt extremely alive and well.

At last, anxious to return to our families, we were ready for the final phase and set off early, with the mules leading. By now we were fully acclimatised, and able to walk steadily up the steep winding path. In the distance we could see our Tibetan guides with the mules who were almost galloping to get home. Soon they disappeared over a ridge high above us. We were not frightened of getting lost, because we followed a clear path ahead which had been made by generations of Buddhist pilgrims who had made this pilgrimage around the sacred mountain. Soon, the steep winding path took us up over ridges where the trees started to thin out. By early afternoon, we had reached another moonscape, and we crossed the pass at about five p.m., with Ying and myself in the lead, and our older friend, accompanied by two Tibetans, several hundred yards in the rear. As the light started to fade, we started to look for the camp which we expected that our Tibetan advance guard had made. The path started to drop steeply, and for an hour or two, we followed the course of an old riverbed while the light faded completely. Eventually, we caught up with the Tibetans, who had arrived a couple of hours earlier, made a huge fire and already eaten their dinner.

Sometime later, when it was completely dark, our friend arrived, riding a mule. He was completely exhausted. When we accused our Tibetans of leaving us behind, they excused themselves by saying that the mules wanted to go home and they couldn't stop them. We believed that. We arrived back at our hotel in Deqin early the following afternoon, after a walk of about six hours down a steep path which wound in and out of a riverbed. Two days later we were back in Kunming, saying goodbye to our friend as he caught a flight back to London via Bangkok, while we took the four-hour flight to Beijing on China Air.

During the trip, Ying and I had decided that our family would return to England in the late summer of 1999. This left me in a quandary. By chance, I had stumbled on a major project of which I had become a key part. Sparkice's success could change a lot of things, and if it worked, would make us rich. Edward depended on my experience and knowledge. Both he and my wife encouraged me to stay in Beijing and continue with the Sparkice project. But I suspected that if I did this, within a year or two our family relationship would have been seriously damaged. An eligible foreigner living in China with his wife and family overseas seems to be catnip to Chinese girls, who prefer married men to singles for a romantic fling or even marriage because they are already 'run in'. I also felt that our children would benefit from having both their parents at home at least some of the time. I decided to return home with my family.

After a twenty-minute conversation with Edward (for him, a long conversation), we decided on a compromise. After organising my family back home in England, I would return to Beijing for a couple of months, to help out while the organisation was restructured. Then, from my base near London, I could promote the Sparkice China-based internet solution to retailers and wholesalers in Europe.

Meanwhile, in November 1999, China signalled that, after fifteen years of negotiations, it had reached agreement with the United States to become a member of the World Trade Organization. The huge, low-cost Chinese labour force had already attracted many major Western retailers to buy and ship labour intensive manufactured products to customers in their stores, from San Diego to Berlin. The WTO agreement accelerated this process, because it brought China within the agreed set of rules which governed international trade, thereby reducing greatly the risk faced by a Western company in China. Sparkice's concept of automating the process of international trade by placing it online seemed now to be the right solution at just the right time.

Large companies are conservative animals. Products sold by large retailers have often been bought by them from the same manufacturing company for many years. Purchasing relationships are built up over time, and are hard to change. But we were confident that our process would be compelling, because it would provide much greater efficiency and lower cost, once it was operating.

That, of course, was the question. Could Sparkice develop a smooth and reliable operating solution? Already Edward had spent millions of the new money to hire software engineers. They had been set to work to develop the thousands of lines of code which would emerge on a computer screen as a series of panels, starting with an enquiry from a Western buyer through a negotiation to a completed sale, all done over the internet. Several years earlier, I had been involved in a major computer programme while I was in the City, which had run over in time and cost by more than one hundred per cent, because the program users had not provided a clear design blueprint to the computer programmers who were writing the algorithms in code. I could see the same problem here. Many people, including Edward, believed that the programmers were the designers, and once twenty highly qualified and highly paid programming experts were sitting in front of their computer screens, the system problem was solved. Software code is an intricate web of logical relationships, so changing code in mid-stream creates a complicated problem. One change in one line of code can affect hundreds or thousands of other logical relationships within the whole programme. Hence, all the design work had to be completed, in detail, before starting on the code. The unfortunate story of most computerisation projects is that design gets mixed up with coding and implementation. In this respect, Sparkice was no different to most other organisations.

After a year or so of increasing cash outflow and frustration, Sparkice ended up spending two million dollars on an off-the-shelf software solution provided by a major American software company called Ariba. This package had then to be adapted, with Ariba's help, to Sparkice's needs. By now, Sparkice had learned that the fundamental problem wasn't the software. It was the design, or what the software was supposed to do. Belatedly, this was addressed in a series of long meetings, to some of which I was a party by phone six thousand miles away in our house in the countryside near London.

If this sounds amateurish and incompetent, it was, but no more so than most large computer projects. An expert writing in an English computer magazine a few years ago stated that less than one-fifth of large computer design projects are successfully realised. In *The Prince*, Machiavelli's handbook for Italian princes and dukes, he wrote more than four hundred years ago that 'there is nothing more difficult to plan, more doubtful of success nor more dangerous to manage than the creation of a new system'. We at Sparkice did not have a system already, so we were not trying to change it, but just design a new one from scratch, and that meant we did not have to try and put 'new wine into old bottles'. But Machiavelli's comments still applied. The story is often the same — lack of definition of the precise details, while the consultants and computer experts, who get paid per hour or per day for their time, make out like bandits. Sparkice's case was better than many, in that the underlying problem was not lost in the morass of non-communication, misunderstanding and blame avoidance which characterises most computer project disasters. But it was still a huge headache, which soaked up as much as half of the substantial sum of money which Edward, with my help, had raised from investors, mainly in America and Europe. Even then, we had to ditch several of our ideas, like online payment, which were correct in principle, but too early for the technology and for China's foreign exchange regime, still then a high wall separating Chinese financial markets from the rest of the world. The solution we ended up with only satisfied a part of the original concept, by focusing on advertising Chinese exporters online to Western buyers, and assisting with product enquiries. The rest had to be done by the companies involved between each other, although we provided a multilingual helpline.

Still, to get Chinese factories connected at all over the internet to Western buyers in 2001 was some kind of achievement. I was reminded of Doctor Johnson's famous comment about a woman preaching a sermon in church that 'It is not done well, but you are surprised to find it done at all'. In England, I turned from talking to investors, to trying to persuade suspicious supply chain heads of companies like Sainsbury's and Tesco that our revolutionary China-based sourcing solution (for that, in industry parlance, was what it was) could make a huge difference to them. My words fell on receptive ears, because all of them were intent on increasing their volumes of purchasing from China, either directly or via offices in Hong Kong. Their responses varied in terms of enthusiasm. Some, like Sainsbury's, the large British supermarket chain, said the Sparkice idea was interesting. But I never got any follow up from them, and discovered a few years later that they had tried to bring the whole project in-house, but had to write off more than two hundred million pounds when their solution didn't work. Others, like the one-pound store Poundland, only founded a few years before, and humble and small enough to consider using an outside agency like Sparkice, were genuinely enthusiastic. We visited them in their headquarters in the English West Midlands to give a presentation, but their belief in our reliability was dulled when Jordan, who flown over from Beijing the previous day, kept their senior executives, including both their founders, waiting for half an hour while he tried to locate the correct demonstration programme on his laptop.

My role as fundraiser was not quite finished. Edward, who regularly flew around the world to meet existing Sparkice investors and find new ones, asked me one day to collect him at a hotel by the motorway outside London's Heathrow Airport, to drive him to a meeting in the City of London with the head of HSBC, Sir John Bond. Apparently, Sir John had approached Edward after a presentation in Singapore with a view to making an investment in Sparkice. Since then, a team from HSBC had visited the Sparkice office, now occupying a whole floor in a brand-new block in central Beijing. Edward's meeting in London was intended to confirm the result of a board meeting at HSBC the previous day, at which the idea of investing in Sparkice had been discussed. I remember that Edward became extremely nervous as our progress through the London streets was delayed a little by heavy traffic. We arrived a few minutes late, and rushed to the top of the idiosyncratic, blue-windowed building beside the Thames which HSBC used as their London headquarters. Edward needn't have worried. The great man quickly emerged from an office, shook Edward's hand, and told him that he had the ten million dollars which they had discussed previously. Then I was introduced to Sir John, who was quite short, with penetrating brown eyes, and silver hair over his collar, and his chief financial officer, a quiet, solid-looking man who said little (and later became the chairman of HSBC). As the owner of a tiny stake myself in Sparkice, I felt reassured that one of the world's major banks had become a substantial shareholder in the company.

Edward was, understandably, in an ebullient mood as we drove back along the motorway from London to Heathrow Airport, from where he was flying to Munich for a meeting with his German mentor, Werner Gauch, before returning to Beijing. Hs ability to convince investors of his vision had impressed me from the beginning — after all, it had only taken him ten minutes to convince me. But to extract ten million dollars from one of the world's major banks, one renowned for its conservatism, for a project as visionary and unreal as Sparkice, was a remarkable achievement. In the car, as we discussed the business, I got some hints which explained Edward's nervousness. The money raised so far, about twenty million dollars, had nearly all gone, and keeping a staff of two hundred people in one of Beijing's most expensive office locations would quickly soak up a million or two more. On the other side of the ledger, a few hundred Chinese companies were paying for appearance fees to advertise their wares to foreign buyers, but these amounted to less than a million dollars a year. The only way for Sparkice to succeed was to cut its costs drastically. Letting half its people go was a start, and moving from the very expensive office to somewhere less fashionable and much cheaper was step two. But any mention of this approach drew a stony silence from Edward. I imagined that this was a topic which had occupied several recent board meetings. I think Edward believed that he could go on raising money, even from the public on a stock exchange, until either the business got to breakeven and stopped burning cash, or he was able to take advantage of the 'greater fool principle' by cashing out some of his shares at a good price.

On the way back home from Heathrow, after dropping Edward off for his Munich flight, my reflections were sober. The buoyant stock market of the dotcom boom had turned to bust. The public appetite to buy shares in any kind of technology sounding company had been founded on the expectation that the share price would be higher next month. When the direction of travel reversed, and share prices started to fall, investor sentiment changed radically. It was as if a switch had been turned off. Suddenly, no one wanted to touch a dotcom company with a long pole. Even profitable companies like eBay were having a difficult time persuading their shareholders of their bright future. I reflected that Edward's dream of getting Sparkice to the public share market was pie in the sky.

What about the alternative — the long haul of turning the company into a viable business? This would certainly take a few more years, and meanwhile, Sparkice could husband carefully its new ten million dollars. But my car journey with Edward had given me a fresh glimpse into his mind. The hubris created by television interviews and invitations to prestigious events had overtaken him. Edward had become master of all he surveyed. There was no way that he would countenance a pullback which could damage his image. Probably he also thought that pulling in his horns would damage his credibility and seriously impact on his ability to raise new cash.

When I heard, a month or two later, that a palace coup at Sparkice led by Jordan, the Canadian lawyer, to remove Edward as CEO had failed, I knew the writing was on the wall. Was it time to brush off and revive my ideas about a China focused financial services company?

Meanwhile, through contacts at the British Embassy in Beijing which we had acquired through our work, we were granted a visa for our Chinese nanny from Beijing to come with us when we returned to England. She spent a year with us as a nanny in the English countryside, where her upbringing as a Chinese peasant in Shandong province in north-eastern China proved to be extremely useful in gardening. She looked after our dogs, a Pekinese and a spaniel (no prizes for guessing which one ran that show) and looked after our children, where she became expert at board games like Monopoly and Risk although she could not read or speak English. She can't ever have seen anything like our English household in her life, but settled in quickly, demonstrating the extraordinary ability of the Chinese to adapt and thrive in any situation. She even managed to get herself into a picture taken by the local newspaper of a visit by Prince Charles to our local village. But she had left behind in her village in China a much older husband and her young son, and had to return back home when her visa expired. She was sorely missed by all of us, especially the dogs who spent several days waiting by our front door after she left, waiting for her to walk in.

A small part of the millions which Sparkice had raised found its way into my salary, and I was generously remunerated for striving to spread Sparkice's gospel amongst the multinational retailing community in Europe. Meanwhile, while our peasant nanny from Shandong played Monopoly with our children and I took them to school and back, my energetic wife had started working in the City to advise fund managers in London and the rest of Europe on developments in an emerging China share market which would obviously become significant. Ying quickly established herself as one of the people in London's financial market who really knew about China. In the world of the City, where correct information and accurate expectations are worth millions, her advice became increasingly sought after. She realised that there was a small but growing number of Chinese companies whose shares were listed on the stock market, and which needed to raise large additional amounts of capital to fund their fast growing businesses. Their problem was that they usually spoke little or no English, and did not understand how foreign investors based in places like London, New York, Geneva and Milan would perceive them. They seized on Ying as their guide. She was in a strong position to operate as an intermediary between Chinese private entrepreneurs who wanted to raise capital, and foreign portfolio managers who were in the business of investing it, but knew hardly anything about China.

As my hopes for Sparkice began to fade, I began talking to Ying about the business she was creating. We realised that this could be an opportunity for us to combine our China knowledge with our start-up experience. If we could find a backer, we could become first movers in an area in which we had a real advantage, in a market which was growing fast. I started casting around for financiers who might be interested in participating in such a venture. Ideally, we needed to collaborate with an existing bank or securities company which had the substantial capital which we needed to trade with investment institutions, plus the range of operating licences which would allow us to be accepted by the increasingly tough financial regulator. It was quite a tall order, but I knew that the City is nothing if not highly entrepreneurial, and anything which had a money smell would attract someone.

My instincts were correct. We had a couple of false starts, one with a Swedish bank which had just sold its operation in Russia to one of the large global investment banks and thought, for a time, of repeating the trick in China, and another with an Australian bank which wanted to penetrate the China market from its base in Sydney. After both of these promising initiatives fell flat, I decided to change my tack. Maybe it would be better to stay nearer home, and look for a British based securities company as our partner. We visited a banker friend in London. She reeled off a list of names.

One by one, I went through these. I had an excellent conversation over the phone with the CEO of the first one, but when I called back a week later, his secretary told me he had been fired the day before, and had left the company. At the next one, I was referred to a member of the banking team. After a short telephone conversation, we arranged a meeting. This went well, and so a few days later we were sitting in front of the CEO of the bank, a massively tall former rugby player who towered over everyone. A former banker, with a couple of colleagues, he had acquired an underperforming, middle ranking investment bank during the dotcom boom, using hugely inflated paper in his listed company as the acquisition currency. Like us, he was a go-getter. I repeated my story, and I could see immediately that he had been well briefed, and already knew something about both of us. I started to get a warm feeling.

It took a few more months and several more meetings, but we had found our banking partner in London.

VII

BANKING ON CHINA

The rugby player was the driving force in the organisation we had joined. He relied on two henchmen. It wasn't long before we met them. One was an accountant in his mid to late thirties, with an Oxford degree in mathematics, who had worked for some blue chip names before joining forces with the rugby player. The other was much older, I guessed in his mid-fifties who, I was told, had been brought into the organisation to get rid of a large number of bankers after the acquisition, something that the other two members of the team had found difficult. I thought of them as the rugby player, the accountant and the hitman. It was important for me to work out who the decision maker was. I guessed that if two out of the three decided on something, then it became a decision. (This turned out to be the case.) I targeted the rugby player and the accountant because I felt they would be happy to see us succeed. I wasn't so sure about the hitman. I decided that we had to be careful with him.

Together with our new colleagues, we set up a new company, a subsidiary of the listed bank, to focus on business in China. The bank owned a majority stake of this new company, and we owned a minority, leaving some shares over which we could use to give to talented people, to persuade them to jump ship from their large, safe organisations, and join our potentially volatile journey. We discussed who, in our new organisation, should do what. The rugby player was surprised when I told him that Ying would be the CEO, and that I would return to Shanghai to establish a research office in Pudong which would act as our ears, eyes and client recruitment office. I already had a Chinese friend who had worked for Softbank in Shanghai, who I knew would be keen to join us in Pudong as the first Chinese employee.

True, this arrangement did appear counterintuitive. Ying was the Chinese expert, and I had more experience as a manager. But there were two good reasons for my decision. We were going to become an international bank (albeit a very small one), and Chinese clients liked to talk from China directly to someone Chinese who was based in London, six thousand miles away. In China, there were many thousands of people like Ying, but in London, hardly any. Here, she would stand out as a major asset for our business, because we were selling global knowhow to people whose horizons stopped at Shanghai and Beijing.

Secondly, by now our children were at weekly boarding school in England. If there was only one parent to whom the children came home to each weekend, we thought it better that this should be their mother. We thought this was a good compromise which allowed both of us to take advantage of this new, exciting opportunity which had appeared.

The corporate paperwork for the new company was completed, and off we went — all two of us, who with the triumvirate mentioned earlier made up the board. We immediately needed more good people. Ying had an Indian friend we had worked with a few years before, who was an experienced City banker. As it happened, she wasn't doing anything, and decided to throw her lot in with us. We found someone from our partner to run our back office trade settlements and compliance function. With my young friend in Shanghai, who was called Jim, that made five: in London, two women, one Chinese and the other Indian, with a British man in the back office, and in Shanghai, a young Chinese, fresh out of business school, and a tall Englishman. Our multicultural Sino-British organisation fitted nicely into an increasingly multicultural London.

I flew from London back to Shanghai, rented a nice apartment in the middle of old Shanghai, in the quarter called Puxi, met up with my Chinese assistant Jim, and started looking for office space. As in 1989, it was a good time to invest in China, because the Asian financial crisis which had started in 1997, followed by the SARS epidemic in 2003, had sapped confidence in the country, and had driven away the foreign investors and the banks. Premium office space was cheap in Shanghai. Once again, Chinese companies desperately needed foreign capital and recognition. I found Chinese landlords falling over themselves to attract us. I was able to rent quickly a small office in the tallest building in Shanghai (it has since been overtaken by two other even taller buildings which stand next to it).

The Shanghai Government had laid the foundations for this building at the height of the mid-1990s boom as a flagship of the new Pudong development zone, and then had been forced to go slow on construction as the market for tenants collapsed during the Asian crisis. But defying the naysayers, they had pushed ahead and finished the building, which was now beginning to fill up. I wondered why the office tenant take-up was so slow, and discovered, eventually, that, unfortunately, a number of Chinese workers had been killed during construction, and the building had acquired some notoriety amongst the superstitious Chinese. A story was circulated that men had died during construction because its enormous height had disturbed the dragons which lived in the clouds.

Bravely, Hyatt had set up a spectacular hotel at the top of the building, above the forty-eighth floor, with views which stretched over the whole city, and beyond. Our office was only on the twenty-third floor, but its windows still gave us a fine view over the river and far into the old part of Shanghai. My Chinese colleague Jim told me that just after the very tall building had been completed a couple of years earlier, an unemployed carpenter from northern China had decided to see if he could climb the outside of the building all the way to the top. And he did. Apparently on the way down, he was coaxed inside a window, and then taken away in a police van.

A Chinese friend of ours had attended Oxford University in the late 1980s on a graduate course as a government sponsored scholar, and we had met him in London at that time. Now, he was based in Shanghai as a senior manager for one of the largest Chinese securities firms. He introduced us to his CEO in Shanghai. It turned out that this Chinese broking firm had hundreds of Chinese companies as clients who sought external capital. These companies were keen to be taken outside the stifling Chinese environment, into the fresh air of the global market for capital and ideas, and they wanted foreign shareholders. At that time, most capital in China was allocated by the Chinese Government via the banking system. There had been a sudden, but short lived burst of interest from foreign investors in Chinese offshore registered startups around the dotcom boom of 1998 to 1999, but those days had passed. We thought we saw an opportunity. We grabbed it with both hands, a commercial agreement was made between our small company and the much larger Chinese one, tasty Chinese spirits were consumed, and we sat back to see what would happen.

We did not have to wait very long. Within a few days, the first introduction from our Chinese partners arrived, and I found myself in a car travelling from Shanghai to Hangzhou, to meet a Chinese entrepreneur who had started his own company making cars. Like most of China's entrepreneurs, he was from a simple, or peasant background. He had grown up in Zhejiang province in the Yangtse basin, had started his business career twenty years before by making refrigerators, and had then progressed to motorcycles, in which field he had quickly become one of the largest manufacturers in China.

But what he really wanted to do was make cars. Six years previously, he had started to try and achieve his unrealistic sounding ambition. The result was that the previous year, he had sold about twenty thousand cars to poor Chinese as their first car, at prices around four or five thousand dollars each. The market he understood and aimed at was the Chinese household's first car, for which he competed fiercely with many other home-grown Chinese auto manufacturers, and which he knew lay some way off the radar screen of every foreign car company, whose products lay far beyond the pocket of most Chinese households at that time. The great Chinese real estate boom, which has enriched China's middle class enormously, was only just starting, and Chinese households, although they saved ferociously, were still very hard up. The man's name was Mr Li Shu Fu.

I didn't hold out a lot of hope for this project, but it was our first business introduction from our Chinese business partners. I thought it would have been rude not to follow it up, and politeness is a key consideration in China. Also, I liked the beautiful city of Hangzhou, and its cuisine. It was where I had met the Chinese director of tourism fifteen years earlier.

I had not travelled outside Shanghai for a few years. The terrible traffic jams in the city had been eased by the completion of enormous, swooping overpasses carried on tall concrete pillars over the city's residential suburbs. This was the inner city ring-road financed partly by the corporate vehicle Shanghai Industrial Holdings which had been established as a company listed on the Hong Kong Stock Exchange. Once out of the city, instead of driving on a crowded single-lane road blocked with large, overloaded lorries, we sped along a new expressway to Hangzhou. The car company's headquarters lay in the industrial suburbs. The factory premises were dominated by a building about four hundred yards long. Obviously this was where the cars were made. As I drove up, everything struck me as looking clean and well organised.

We signed in at the front gate, and were directed to a multi-storey office block, where we entered a large room on the ground floor. Sitting at a large table were several smartly dressed Chinese men. These were the would-be tycoon's financial advisor and his assistants. He had been hired by the car magnate to advise him on the best way to raise fifty million dollars — a lot of money for a car company which had been going for only four years, and whose products could best be described as 'inexpensive'. His first words to me were, "Who are you? We are already in discussions with Goldman Sachs and Deutsche Bank and we don't need any more help."

At this point, I realised that I had only a minute or two to put my best foot forward. I explained that I had been involved for many years in China business, I reeled off some statistics about the Chinese car market which I had looked up the day before, and I said I knew a number of investors based in London and elsewhere who would be very interested in supporting Mr Li's plans for expansion. The last part was an exaggeration, but sometimes you have to paint a picture, then trust to your own skill and good fortune that you can make it come true. The advisor seemed impressed by my speech, and we were allowed to sit down.

Having got over the first hurdle, we started discussing some of the details. These were important because, I told them, I would write a report which would be sent to hundreds of foreign investors and which would attract investor attention in Europe and the United States to Mr Li and his company. This part was true. My request to visit the factory was denied, apparently because visitors were not allowed when it was in operation. When I looked over the cars which were sitting outside waiting to be taken to showrooms, I realised that Mr Li probably didn't want to me to see some of the manufacturing processes he was using. How had he been able to develop a car production line without assistance from a Western car company? Apparently, he had hired overseas consultants to advise him. It was a remarkable achievement, but I suspected that many tasks which would have been performed by a machine at Volkswagen's factory in Wolfsburg in Germany, or in GM's at Red River in Detroit, were being performed here by several men. I knew the consequence would be lack of precision, in an industry where a difference of one micron — one-thousandth of a centimetre — makes a critical difference to engine wear, efficiency and safety. Mr Li's cars might be price competitive, but they could not come near to matching the quality offered by the multinational brands, or even the better capitalised and more experienced Chinese car producers.

When I met the founder of the car factory, Mr Li, I began to understand how he could have achieved what seemed impossible. He was able to lay out an ambitious and compelling roadmap clearly and succinctly. Mr Li was about forty years old, of medium height, with a high forehead and bright eyes. After thanking me for my visit, he explained that his vision was to bring affordable cars to the Chinese masses which would, he said, start to become prosperous within a few years. He hoped to use this platform to expand into a wide range, including luxury models which would be in demand as Chinese households became wealthier. His vision in the longer term was to create a Chinese auto company of global scale and competitiveness. He said that foreign car manufacturers had not offered him cooperation because they feared creating an effective Chinese competitor. Looking closely at me, he said that he had heard that the British car company Rover was looking for Chinese partners. Could I help him to talk to them? I replied that I would be delighted to investigate the opportunity and make an introduction, but I did not recommend Rover as a partner, as I thought their technology was out of date and their management had stripped the company of whatever inspiration it might once have had. He nodded, as if to agree with me, but I don't think that my words persuaded him to abandon his search for Rover. Mr Li's Rover dream was only terminated when a government owned car company, Nanjing Auto, acquired Rover, and then shipped its production lines, screw by screw, to Nanjing. Nanjing Auto was acquired by Shanghai Auto. Today, the Chinese version of Rover is a mid-size saloon which competes with Audi and BMW, and carries the name REWE on its bonnet, together with a crest in red, gold and black. It's a more competitive car than anything which Rover in Birmingham, England made since 1970, when communist unions effectively hijacked the company.

We finished off the proceedings with a dinner in a nearby hotel overlooking the famous West Lake in Hangzhou. I knew the meeting had gone well when the financial adviser produced a bottle of Chinese spirits which we proceeded to finish. I returned to Shanghai with a mandate to raise fifty million dollars for Mr Li, jointly with another, major investment bank.

Mr Li had the last laugh on Nanjing Auto, which beat him to acquire the British car company Rover. He has become a major force in the global auto industry, buying the famous Swedish car manufacturer Volvo from Ford in 2009 and turning it round, then acquiring the company which makes black London taxicabs in 2013, the British Lotus cars in 2017, and ten per cent of the German company Daimler in 2018. I can't say that I foresaw all this when I met him in September 2003, but I certainly did recognise him then as an individual of integrity and vision who probably had the courage and drive to bring his ambitious dreams to reality. I think it was that perception of him that enabled me to turn persuasively to the foreign investment community on his behalf.

After my visit, I arranged for him to visit London with his team, where he was introduced by Ying and her Indian colleague to British fund managers who, I suspect, were in equal part suspicious and intrigued. Mr Li got his fifty million dollars. He spent it well. We couldn't have asked for a better start to our new undertaking.

It was interesting to compare Shanghai with the city I had lived in eight years earlier. Many of the high-rise cranes were still there, but they had moved out of the city centre into remoter areas. The suburbs which the Shanghai vice mayor had described to me and my guest in 1996 had taken shape, and there were convenience stores and pharmacies springing up to serve them, but with Chinese, not English, names on them. In the city centre, there was a new sheen. Green public spaces and pedestrian areas had started to replace the narrow, grimy streets, cars had mostly replaced the ubiquitous bicycles, and Shanghai's subway system had been extended from two to ten lines. The city sucked in students, migrant workers, ambitious hopefuls and seasoned executives from all over China, and beyond. Eight years earlier, everyone I had met in Shanghai was a local. Now, it was quite unusual to come across native Shanghainese who had been born and had grown up in the city. Although Shanghai had to be careful of not upsetting the party bosses in Beijing, who remained sensitive about successful Shanghai's potential independence from the rest of China, the city wanted to demonstrate that it was an international city, and an Asian leader of the not so distant future. It encouraged as many manifestations of foreign culture as it could think of. The range of international cuisine already rivalled Hong Kong. On an average day one could already see most of the luxury car marques of the developed country car makers. Large Mercedes were everywhere, Ferraris and Maseratis not uncommon, and the noisily exuberant exhaust roar of a Lamborghini could be occasionally heard.

The change in the Shanghai people's mindset was dramatic. Eight years before, no one had owned real estate and by any standard, everyone in Shanghai was still poor, meaning that the savings of the wealthiest probably amounted no more than ten thousand dollars at most. Now, a well-defined spending class had emerged, driven probably by the beginnings of the huge Chinese real estate boom (property prices rose by between fifty and eighty times in local currency terms in tier one and tier two Chinese cities between 2003 and 2015). The attitude to foreigners had changed, from ill-disguised envy to frank interest, or in some cases, indifference. I found it stimulating that Shanghai was arriving as an equal to other great world cities, although the lack of a presiding genius of urban design, like Baron Haussmann in Paris, was sometimes evident.

I remember in 1994 attending a lecture in London which was given by the famous British architect Sir Richard Rogers on the design work he had done for the

Shanghai Government in the early 1990s for the new development area of Pudong, which lay across the river from the famous Bund area. His overriding vision was to link the Huangpu River which divides Shanghai with the new city of Pudong, by creating a pedestrian only green area next to the river, and keeping cars and lorries to well defined expressways further back. The Shanghainese thanked him for his proposal, and did the opposite, bringing tall buildings and their access roads right down to the river, which they walled off from the traffic areas. The result of this layout today is that the Lujiazui zone next to the river in Shanghai on the Pudong side is known by everyone as somewhere you don't go with a car, because it's one big traffic jam and there's not enough parking. Everyone I know walks or takes public transport when they go to Lujiazui. The Shanghainese should just have followed Rogers' advice.

But that's the thing. The Chinese want to do it their way — and why shouldn't they, even when they mess it up, like the Shanghai Government did with the design of the Lujiazui new zone? China is Chinese, and their way needn't necessarily be the wrong way. A lot of American economists, some of whom I know, still haven't come to terms with the fact that China doesn't want to become like America. Nor does China want America to become like China, even if America could. China is happy to be China and to let America be America.

I was inspired by the meeting in Hangzhou with Mr Li, because it validated my hypothesis that Chinese entrepreneurs, like him, were the driving force behind China's dramatic economic emergence. Mr Li controlled his company through another corporate vehicle based in the British Virgin Islands, about which it was difficult to get accurate information. I knew that he held the controlling interest, but the other shareholders and the source of much of his finance were only to be guessed at. It requires a significant sum to build two car production plants, each four hundred feet long. Knowing that Chinese entrepreneurs often partner with local governments, I thought that local officials, the people who could smooth his way with licences and introductions to local state owed banks, must be his partners. I knew also that Mr Li had also been working closely with a Hong Kong based entrepreneur of Chinese origin, age about forty-five, who had made a small fortune in real estate and was leveraging that as a one-man corporate finance fixer for Chinese entrepreneurs like Mr Li. When Mr Li flew to London to meet the Western fund managers who financed him, this fixer came along. We were surprised at his sophistication and awareness. The large success fee which he earned from Mr Li for listing his company in Hong Kong created a good basis for our relationship with him, and he remains a good friend of ours. The Chinese never forget such personal stories and relationships.

At the first board meeting of our new bank held in London, the rugby player, the accountant and the hitman were expecting a modest progress report from us. But our fees from Mr Li's deal covered our operating costs for several months. They were certainly surprised, possibly impressed. We decided to expand. Within a year, we had twenty people working in our two offices.

Times had changed in the City. The firms which had employed people whose fathers they had been to school with had largely disappeared. In a highly expansionary period for financial markets, London had become one of the key global finance hubs. The City had expanded by ten or twenty times, and in the process, had sucked in people and capital from all corners of the Earth. An ambitious and well-presented accountant from Sri Lanka, Madrid, Moscow or Marseilles who did a one-year course at one of the London colleges could expect to have several attractive City job offers before he or she left school. The environment was therefore extremely dynamic and multicultural. Nine-to-five work hours had changed to six in the morning until eight at night, something I blamed the Americans for. They wear long working hours as a badge of pride because, for them, it indicates commitment and demand for your time. It was not uncommon, even, to find people coming in to work all weekend.

The thing that was missing, though, was trust. In the old days, your lunch might last three hours, with enough alcohol to make returning to the desk in the afternoon a hazardous exercise. But in the process, deals were done, information exchanged, and relationships strengthened. Displaying bad faith, or reneging on a promise made verbally, was considered as a serious offence. The offender was punished by being 'sent to Coventry' (in other words, being ignored). News of bad faith spread fast, and perpetrators found themselves being shut out of deals and conversations. This convention, which had grown up over several hundred years in the City amongst its trading people, was a very useful and congenial way of getting business done quickly and well.

Now, though, things were radically different. The shared values which had made possible the convention of good faith were no longer present. Good faith had been replaced, largely, by the desire to become rich, in its most unconfined form. In a single day one might find oneself discussing information, news or transactions with people from five or more different countries. Everything important which was agreed had to be put in writing. Even then, the lawyers often had to be called in as one party or another decided that it would be cheaper to pay a financial settlement out of court for reneging on a written commitment, than to go ahead with a piece of business which was starting to look negative for their bottom-line.

Lawyers were everywhere. The fastest growing area of law in London was employment law. American banks had started the trend of laying off people, sometimes whole floors of people, at zero notice, and many City banks had followed suit. The famous 'sack' had been replaced with a black plastic bag and a box to carry books out of the building. Work files had to be left behind, and woe betide any employee who, given his dismissal notice, tried to sneak off with a valuable list of clients or the details of a half-finished transaction. Resentful employees often took their employers to court for unfair dismissal, and could win large damages if the ex-employer had not followed the correct dismissal procedure or had acted in a bullying or unfair manner. Such cases were usually settled before they reached a judge, because the bank would pay handsomely to avoid the possibility of a newspaper covering a high profile court case, unless the bank believed its case was overwhelmingly strong.

It took me a month or two to understand this new world. I had found the old system hidebound and class ridden. The multicultural, open City world to which I returned was like a breath of fresh air. But it was not difficult to hire people whom we would term 'rotten apples', troublemakers who often disturbed their colleagues, knew their rights, and were aggressive in defending them, and it was difficult to remove these people, once they had arrived. We had to learn to become very careful about accepting personal references at face value, because providers of bad references faced the risk of court action, if the person in question found out that a poor reference had denied someone a position which they were seeking.

The creation of a harmonious and collaborative working environment within our small enterprise was made more difficult by the new City working environment which favoured self over loyalty and teamwork. We started with five people, in two offices, in London (opposite the Bank of England) and Shanghai (in Pudong's tallest building). After six months we had ten, and after twelve months we had over twenty. In a people-based environment which was spread over two locations six thousand miles apart, I spent much time and energy on attempting to establish bonds of trust and mutual respect which could facilitate the winning and execution of business. But my efforts met only with a modicum of success. Part of the reason was because the City culture did not encourage togetherness. In the highly competitive, dog-eat-dog atmosphere which prevailed, people's natural distrust of each other was encouraged. The cosy chumminess which had prevailed thirty years earlier, when senior partners gave jobs to the sons of people they had been at school with, was no more. Another part lay in the fact that our partners seemed to encourage discord in our ranks. The head of our back office, a close friend of the accountant who was a member of our partner's management team, had been recruited from within our partner's organisation. Everything we discussed in our office was relayed back to our partners, who I think became somewhat alarmed when, within a month of starting, we completed a transaction which covered our start-up costs, with a lot left over. They felt that we might get out of control, and they had to plot ways to control us. Success is a two edged sword, and brings its own problems, one of which is jealousy from outsiders, especially those who feel threatened by a change in the status quo. From early on I felt that our partners were in two minds about our success, given the possibility that we, a successful subsidiary focused on China, could probably attract more interest from the outside investing world than they, the parent company could. Still, no one ever said that it was easy to start a China focused bank. Whatever the problems we faced, I appreciated nevertheless our partner's support, for without it we would have had nothing.

Investment banks attract clients by providing good advice and connections to companies and investing institutions, and they make money from helping their clients to raise capital, invest successfully and pursue their corporate goals, which often include acquiring other companies or disposing of unwanted subsidiaries. In Shanghai, I needed to create an image which could allow our new, very small company to stand out from the many other famous banks based around the world with whom we competed. We certainly could not compete on numbers of people, or on capital. But I thought we could compete with everyone on knowledge of the China market, and we knew a few significant members of the investment management communities in London and elsewhere in Europe.

I decided the best way to raise our public profile was by writing a report on a topic which was interesting and different, while being relevant and money-making. From my earlier experience with Sparkice (which I described in the previous chapter), I knew and understood something about the Chinese internet environment. Already there were several Chinese internet companies whose shares were publicly quoted, either on the Hong Kong or American NASDAQ stock exchanges. Investing institutions were starting to show a little interest in this completely new sector, but very few knew much about it. I also noticed that none of the well-known banks were covering this nascent field.

I encouraged my assistant Jim to look into the activities of these internet companies in China. With typical Chinese diligence, within a few weeks he had assembled a lot of information about them which he sourced from the Chinese internet, from his friends, and from visits to the companies in question. Most international banks had closed their offices in China during the Asian financial crisis and the SARS epidemic, and laid off their China analysts, because there was little or no investor demand for their services. The Chinese internet companies were delighted to find a stock analyst like Jim who wanted to talk to them.

Jim was a thirty-year-old Chinese man who personified the characteristics of his type. He had grown up in Dalian, the northern coastal Chinese town nearest to Japan, had graduated from a good Chinese university, and subsequently from the top-ranked China European business school in Shanghai, a 1994 joint venture between the Shanghai Government and the European Union. I had met him when he was working in Shanghai as an analyst for the Japanese technology investment company Softbank, who had let him go around 2001 when the length and depth of the Asian financial crisis had started to affect their business. I told him about my ideas. He was interested, and trusted me enough to wait until we had established our joint venture project. When I arrived in Shanghai a year or more later, there he was waiting for me. Such is the strength of the personal relationship in China. His presence made the establishment of a local company and an office much easier. He was very loyal, and family-minded, two qualities which I have often found in Chinese people, especially those from the northern part of the country. He was a great partner to have, and I was able to teach him something about the fundamentals of market and stock analysis. He ended up eventually taking these skills and his deep knowledge of China's technology sector to a hedge fund which he started in Shanghai a few years later, and which has become very successful.

Jim's fact-based research formed the core of a long report on China's burgeoning internet sector which I wrote over the Christmas period, and which was published in London in January 2004, and distributed to a wide range of investing institutions based in the main European financial centres. As I had hoped, the report surprised and interested some of the large investing institutions with whom we hoped to do business. They began to reward us by using our services to buy and sell shares in the market, on which we charged sales commission, and one even sent us a large cheque as a payment for our report. For an investing institution which handles thousands of millions of dollars, and which receives income annually in the tens or hundreds of millions, a payment of tens of thousands of dollars is small, in comparison to the daily price movements to which its investments are subject each and every day. Information and ideas which make a real difference to its management of these large amounts are rewarded handsomely, and this is one reason why investment banking can be such a lucrative business.

I had taken an office in Shanghai with room for several people. To start with, Jim and I occupied it by ourselves. Now, I thought it was time to multiply. Through a local head-hunter I found a Chinese office manager who was working for a Japanese company. After a long negotiation, during which she beat me down successively and successfully on her salary, pension and holiday rights, I finally persuaded her to join us. Then I found an American accountant who had previously worked for a Hong Kong based brokerage firm which had drawn its horns in during the Asian crisis. He was happy to re-join the world of securities research. Later when I left Shanghai to return to my family in London, he became head of the office in Shanghai. This group of four formed the foundation of our Shanghai team, which over the next several years tripled in size, moving to a much larger office in the same building.

Jim introduced me to an American lawyer whom he had met earlier, while we were back in Europe, trying to get our project off the ground. The New York based lawyer, another Jim, who had had become involved in an advisory capacity some years earlier with a Chinese project which he had taken over and was trying to finance. American Jim, the lawyer from New York, sat down at our meeting table while he explained his project to me. It sounded extremely complicated, as only a Chinese project can, with several changes of ownership and many characters flitting in and out. My first reaction was to dismiss it as unrealistic, over-complicated, unlikely to succeed and a waste of time. But I took a good look at the lawyer, who was obviously intelligent and of some standing, wore glasses, had mostly white hair and seemed honest. I decided to spend more time on it.

The story started several years earlier, with a Chinese state owned company, Everbright, which had support at the highest level of the Chinese Government, wishing to exploit the booming Chinese mobile phone market, but prohibited from becoming a phone operator by the phone operating monopoly operated by China Telecom. So Everbright decided to become a mobile phone seller instead, opening stores around China and becoming a distributor of the mobile phones made by Nokia, Motorola, Sony and other companies, some Chinese. With little experience in managing a fast-growing retail business in a highly competitive market, Everbright's mobile phone business started to lose a lot of money. The Chinese decided they needed foreign help and cash, and started to look around for a foreign partner.

Meanwhile, an American public company called Greg Manning Auctions, which operated online auctions in collectibles like stamps, had started to think of tapping into China, as the largest collectibles market in the world. The Americans hired two young Chinese executives who had graduated from a leading American business school. These two came up with the idea of combining Everbright's physical phone store network in China with the American company's expertise in online collectible auctions, so that the Chinese online stamp auctions would be supported by a physical, on-the-ground network. The Americans supported the idea, and signed a deal with Everbright whereby they acquired a majority share of the loss-making Chinese store network, in return for providing millions of dollars of new capital and assuming Everbright's debt obligations. A year later, the Americans had wired several million dollars over to China, but the monthly losses were growing. Worried, the Americans decided at a board meeting that something had to be done. But what? This is where Jim, the lawyer sitting in front of me in Shanghai, entered the story. As a board member of Greg Manning Associates, Jim agreed to visit China, to investigate and recommend the best course of action.

When he reached China, Jim found an operation which was out of control, with an expanding network of store locations in the east of China, each of which was losing more and more money. The options that Jim suggested were: invest more, close it all down, or sell it. Most of the Greg Manning board wanted to close it all down, but a large Spanish collectibles company who had recently acquired a large stake in Greg Manning Auctions were reluctant to do this. They did a deal with Jim: the Spanish would support Jim if he could find a way to clean up the Everbright business and find a future for it. Jim's reward would be a large equity stake in the Chinese business.

It was quite easy for Jim to persuade Greg Manning Auctions to give up their stake, but Everbright was a harder sell. Eventually, however, he was able to change the ownership structure so that he was in charge, backed by the Spanish. Cleaning up the business was a tougher proposition. The two young Chinese MBAs who had led the charge to a nationwide distribution network which sold phones and collectibles had to go. In one case, this proved problematic, because the woman in question held the company chop, and refused to give it up without a fight. (In China, the company chop or stamp controls corporate decisions, including access to the company bank account.) When Jim eventually got his hands on the company chop, he was able to access the company bank account. He discovered that substantial funds had been taken from the account. These had been transferred to a private Chinese bank account. A battle ensued, with the Chinese woman threatening to call in friends in Chinese officialdom in her support. But Jim hung tough, and after being threatened with prosecution in the United States, the Chinese party eventually gave in.

Jim's next step was to promote an experienced, honest and capable Chinese executive to the CEO position. Between them, they closed hundreds of stores, leaving a small core in Shanghai which they thought could be turned around. Having cleaned up the business, Jim wanted to recapitalise it and rebuild it. He had started to approach sources of venture capital in China, but with no success. That was where we entered the story.

It was a can of worms, but I knew that the mobile phone business was booming in China. The market was huge. But the phone distribution business was highly competitive, because entry barriers were low. There were other Chinese companies who wanted to tap into this enormous market who were prevented from accessing the mobile operating sector by government regulation, and saw mobile phone distribution as the only way in. But the real problem was thousands of one-store operations. Nevertheless, I felt money could be made and a viable business could be built along the lines of Carphone Warehouse or Phones 4U in the United Kingdom, but only by adopting sophisticated branding and warehousing strategies, and working closely with the telecom operators, as the phone distributors did in the UK.

Our company had the banking credibility and business knowledge to help Jim to raise the capital he needed. In a fish tank which contained some large, aggressive fish with sharp teeth and big appetites, our company was a minnow. We could not hope to compete for juicy projects from high profile clients. The big fish got those. This project, which was the opposite of 'oven-ready', was the kind of project we had to take on. Unpromising though it looked, by repositioning it and adding the backing of ourselves and our London based partner, I thought it had a chance of success. I realised that Jim, the lawyer and board member, lacked much of the business knowledge which was needed. But he had restructured the company, knew where the bodies were buried, understood the legal aspects, and both he and ZG, the Chinese CEO, were completely honest. And ZG had many years of China retail experience working for a major Chinese state-owned conglomerate called China Resources, with part of his time spent in Hong Kong. After I spoke to him, I felt confident we could make it work.

It took eighteen months, but Jim the lawyer's company became our first stock market success in London. After digging deeply into the business, we were able to develop a strong story based on market size and growth, and on the management team based in China. We renamed the company, and after raising two million dollars from private investors, we sold new shares to London based investment institutions on London's second stock exchange called the Alternative Investment Market, or AIM, which had been set up for early-stage growth businesses like this one.

China was full of opportunity. Now we had created a platform, based in London with a reputable banking partner, which gave us an avenue to exploit it.

VIII

EXPERIENCING THE IMPOSSIBLE — MY CLOSE-UP VIEW OF CHINA'S BOOM

From our office window, high up above the city, I could see across the area known as Pudong, which lay across the river from the Shanghai Bund. This had all been farmland in 1988 when I first visited Shanghai, but by 2004 it was covered with buildings, roads and occasionally, a large garden with trees, which one knew immediately had to be a government owned guesthouse or Chinese Communist Party headquarters. Already, Shanghai boasted of many millionaires, but they usually lived in large penthouses at the top of tall apartment buildings, or sometimes in colonial houses in the centre of town, surrounded with high metal gates and high walls topped with barbed wire. Not even the wealthiest and best-connected of the new millionaire class could acquire enough land to own a house with an acre or two or garden. Only the party had that kind of property.

In the far distance, at the other end of Pudong, one could just see the huge new Shanghai airport. When it was built, it seemed too large by a factor of four or five. Now, it's full. At the top of our office building was a hotel, the Hyatt. The building, then one of the tallest in Asia, really was a statement that Shanghai had arrived as a world city, with style and ambition. As a hotel guest, stepping outside one's room on the sixtieth floor, one was treated to a view of twenty floors straight down to the hotel reception. It was like something out of Star Wars. From a hotel window in the early morning it was easy to see the hundreds or thousands of local Chinese residents doing their exercises on the large open spaces either side of the river.

Although much of the hardware and infrastructure in Shanghai had been spectacularly upgraded since my stay there eight years earlier, the people had not changed very much, although immigrants from other parts of China into Shanghai — fortune-hunters as well as peasants looking for building work — had become plentiful. Across the river to the north lay old Shanghai, or Puxi, which remained a city of nooks, corners and crannies, of small streets leading to secluded houses. Here one could drink tea and do business discreetly, sitting perhaps in an ancient garden, in which the washing lines of ten Chinese families had replaced the neatly kept flower beds of colonial yesteryear. Near the east-west running Huangpu River, which divides Pudong to the south from Puxi, lie the large mansions constructed around the turn of the century which had housed the banks and trading houses of late imperial

China. Here is the famous Bund, where goods like tea and silk, shipped downriver from Nanjing and Wuhan, had once been exchanged, on and around the Bund, for Indian opium and European and American manufactured products, all bound for inland China via a network of Chinese merchants known as the Hong.

Prominent among these Bund-based merchant emporia was David Sassoon, a Jew born in Baghdad in 1792 who left Iraq for India, and became a lynchpin of the Indian opium trade which extended in the nineteenth century through east Asia to China. Today, the Sassoon building, a testament to the enormous fortune which the family made from trading in Indian opium, for which China was much the biggest market, overlooks the Huangpu River from its prominent position on the Bund at the junction with Shanghai's main shopping thoroughfare Nanjing Road. When the Communists took it over in 1949, Sassoon's building became the government run Peace Hotel. In recent years it has become part of the Fairmont hotel group, through a joint venture with the Shanghai Government. Near to it stands the pre-war headquarter building of the Hongkong & Shanghai Bank, also seized in 1949 by the Communist Government, becoming eventually the head office of the Pudong Development Bank. Between them is the original Bank of China building, and close by stands the Union Insurance Building, and the Shanghai Club, where foreign expatriates once repaired for refreshment after a day of business on the Bund.

Further back from the Bund stand other large buildings which had in pre-Revolutionary days been banks, merchants' houses or warehouses. Many of these buildings now lie empty, their huge entrances boarded up and locked with chains. Others have been turned into accommodation for Chinese families, or government offices. Further downriver stands an Anglican church, clean and undamaged, doubtless in its day full every Sunday, but now empty, and preserved as a relic of Shanghai's colonial past, of which the city remains proud. Opposite the church stands a rowing club, a charming reminder of a leisured age, but now locked and inaccessible. One could easily imagine young men — doubtless including some well-heeled Chinese - in their colourful blazers mixing with elegant ladies over afternoon tea or a drink. A few yards further on stands a large mansion in its own garden, once the residence of the British consul in Shanghai. The garden contains magnificent mature trees planted a century or more earlier, but part of the house is a museum, while the remainder is empty and boarded up, with slogans in Chinese from the Cultural Revolution reading 'Down with the foreigners' and 'Kill the imperialist running-dogs'.

Such is the colonial furniture of Shanghai, from which it was obvious that the city's idea of itself as the trading entrepot of east Asia was no empty boast. Before World War Two, Shanghai was what it is becoming today: the most dynamic and elegant city not just in China, but in the whole of east Asia.

From the Fairmont Peace Hotel (formerly Sassoon House), one could turn and walk north up Nanjing Road, much of which has been turned into a pedestrian area containing five-star hotels and department stores with international brands from around the world. The Shanghainese took care not to flatten Puxi, where most of Shanghai's best colonial buildings stood, and have modernised it with care. The old street design and houses dating back to the 1900s and before give much of the area its character of a large, close-knit Chinese community, in which everybody knows everyone else's business.

On this earlier urban pattern of blocks of houses divided by alleys and small streets, a modern infrastructure has been superimposed. Every few hundred yards stand subway stations. The Shanghai subway system, which runs on Siemens-designed trains, is state-of-the-art, clean, efficient, and spreads from the city's centre many miles into Shanghai's suburbs, in every direction. The always full buses are electric, and the traffic, in which vehicles made by the Shanghai based joint ventures of Volkswagen and General Motors feature prominently, is extremely busy. On my first trip to Shanghai in spring 1991, I had stayed in the Hilton Hotel, then the only modern hotel in Shanghai's city centre. Twelve years on, I liked to go there occasionally to remind myself of those earlier days, before Shanghai had been rebuilt, when from an upper-floor window on a clear day, one could see the Shanghai suburbs stretching away into the distance toward the old Hongqiao airport a mere ten or fifteen miles away. Behind the Hilton stood the building which in 1920 had housed the first official meeting of the Chinese Communist Party, whose formation had been prompted by Chinese anger at their treatment at the post-war negotiations at Versailles, near Paris, in 1919. The arrangement reached in Versailles between America, France and Britain gave the north-eastern port of Qingdao and part of Shandong province to Japan, instead of restoring it to China, promised earlier as a condition of China's entry into the war on the Allied side in 1917.

Shanghai was where our Chinese banking partners were based. The company was the result of the merger of two Chinese banks in 1997, and was part-owned by the Shanghai Government, which had been required to provide a large part of the new capital in the merger. With this government backing the company formed one of the most powerful investment banking groups in China, with hundreds of branches around China. Many successful Chinese entrepreneurs approached them for assistance with building their businesses. As our Chinese partners did not yet have an office in the United States or in Europe, they turned to us to satisfy their Chinese clients' growing need for exposure to investors and markets in the major developed markets. This appetite for international exposure arose in part from the strict rationing of capital in China for privately owned companies, at that time, and partly from a desire for exposure to foreign expertise and financial markets. There were only a few institutional Chinese investors then; household savings were the largest component of Chinese stock markets, and expectations of the next move in government policy was the main stock market driver, up or down. The government knew which words to use to manipulate the market up or down, and private investors responded to their signals, hoping to anticipate them. Private Chinese companies, of which there were many, some very large, constantly needed fresh capital to expand. But stock listings on China's financial markets were hard to come by, because state owned companies had first dibs at the enormous pool of Chinese savings, either through a stock market listing, or through a loan from one or other of China's state owned commercial banks. Our company's partnership with a large China based investment bank enabled our partners to offer these private Chinese companies new avenues overseas, in London or in Hong Kong, to capital raising. It was an attractive and compelling offer.

Our main contact at our partner's bank was the Chinese friend who had studied at Oxford. He had participated in an organisation which my wife and I had established at that time called the Chinese Economic Association, which was aimed at giving Chinese students in Britain a forum and mouthpiece for their political ideas. Now, fifteen years later, he was a senior manager of this Chinese investment bank, with particular responsibility for supervising the country-wide branch network of offices. He told me that the bank's control systems were not strong enough to prevent some of his bank's branch managers from creaming off substantial sums of money for themselves as side deals in transactions they had arranged with local Chinese enterprises. Indeed, he often looked tense and worried when I met him. No doubt he was under enormous pressure to resolve a huge case of fraud in Sichuan or some other far flung location in mainland China.

I used to play golf with him, at a local private Shanghainese golf club. The joining fee, in those early days, was already about 50,000 American dollars and the annual subscription the same amount, but already it was full, with property developers, bankers like our friend, and Chinese Government officials making up most of the membership. I was always a guest, at our friend's expense (or, more accurately, at the expense of his bank). Today, I'm sure the golf club in Shanghai is still fully subscribed, but I expect that the membership fees have risen exponentially in the years since I last played there. Often we would play with a Beijing government official whose job it was to give official approval to some transaction in which our friend's bank was involved. In a country where the party controlled everything, such approval was usually essential and always desirable. Today, as part of the government's effort to control corruption, members of the Chinese Communist Party are banned from playing golf.

At the same time as I had arrived in Shanghai, our friend's daughter had arrived in England to go to school. While he looked after me in Shanghai, we arranged for his daughter to enter a local English girls' school, from which she eventually graduated to one of the best British universities. After attending graduate school at an American Ivy League college, she is now a qualified psychiatrist working in the United States. Such are the quid pro quos on which Chinese relations depend.

Our friend in the bank was a highly intelligent, civilised and ambitious man with whom I formed a close working relationship. He was rewarded for his task in bringing his bank's branch offices into line by being appointed as the first chairman of his bank's new asset management joint venture with a large German insurance company. Today, he owns several properties in Shanghai and Beijing, and has retired on a large German style pension. From him, I learned a great deal about the true state of the Chinese economy (booming), and the country's investment banking system (closed, corrupt, and full of opportunity). Our friend's insights into the Chinese situation were of great interest to me, because they were much at odds with the outside world's assessment at that time, which expected China to slump back soon into an economic depression.

Our business benefited greatly from its working relationship with our Chinese partners, which was based fundamentally on the personal relationship between our friend and me based in Shanghai, and Ying in London. Our successful efforts for Mr Li Shu Fu and his car company Geely in Hangzhou gave our Chinese partners the confidence to introduce us to more of their Chinese corporate clients. Over the next year, I travelled around eastern China, receiving a first-class education in the ingenuity, drive and success of China's private entrepreneurs.

One such was a privately owned company in northern China which made steel pipes for oil drilling. The business sounds mundane and unexciting, but as oil prices rose in the first decade of the new millennium, exploratory oil drilling expanded dramatically, and the demand for the company's pipes grew exponentially. The company's profits quadrupled and its share price rose more than ten times after the company's shares were listed on the Hong Kong Stock Exchange. The European investors to whom we had introduced the company were delighted.

Another was a privately owned Chinese pharmaceutical company based in the old Chinese imperial city of Nanjing, which had a decent business producing generic drugs like paracetamol and vitamin C, but which wanted to enter the difficult and expensive business of developing its own proprietorial drugs for heart disease. I visited the company several times, to try and get a better understanding of their research. Regrettably, this goal, of developing successful proprietorial research which could pass over the high hurdles of regulatory approval proved to be too much for them. The generic drug business didn't have the profitability which we needed to introduce them successfully to Western investors, and we had to give them a pass.

In Ningbo, a coastal city just south of Shanghai, famous for its seafood, its deep water port and its enterprise, I visited a textile factory, again privately owned, which had prospered by importing the best Swiss textile machinery for spinning and weaving. From producing cloth from cotton grown in western China, where the hot dry climate of Xinjiang province was ideal, the company developed quickly into designing and manufacturing its own branded clothing for ladies and men.

Another Chinese private company, based about two hours south-west of Shanghai in Hangzhou, had developed an alternative mobile phone technology, first used successfully in Japan, which was well suited to densely populated urban centres, of which China had many. The technology had been developed by Chinese engineers who had worked previously for the Japanese company Kyocera, a pioneer in mobile phone technology, before starting their own Chinese business in 1991. The engineers licensed the technology from Japan, then made their own modifications to adapt it for medium-size urban centres in China (meaning populations of between one and five million, of which there are more than one hundred in China). The technology used mobile telephone base stations linked to handsets by radio waves, but at much smaller scale, so that the radius covered by each base station was a few hundred yards, instead of being a couple of miles as in the 2G GSM systems then being used in China. The base stations themselves were much smaller, and could be located inside the attic space of an existing building. The radiation was accordingly much less than in a conventional mobile phone system, using less power and reducing any health risk. The advantage for Chinese telephone operators was that this system was much cheaper and quicker to install than a conventional mobile phone system. The company, which was called UT Starcom, had persuaded its host city Hangzhou, with a population of several million, to adopt the system. Hangzhou city became a demonstration and testing ground, and attracted many smaller and poorer cities in eastern and central China to adopt the company's system — providing UT Starcom with a large market for its product. In 2001, the company had sold shares to the public on the American NASDAQ stock exchange, and the shares had risen sharply on the back of big increases in revenue, strong operating results and the company's exciting prospects.

The problem for UT Starcom was that its novel mobile phone system, based on miniature base stations and low radiation, competed with the mobile phone monopoly operated by Government owned China Mobile, a company which today shares a telecommunications triopoly with its sister companies Unicom and China Telecom. The microsystem also lacked the technical versatility and scope to upgrade to more powerful mobile phone standards, like 3G, which China at that time was planning to introduce as the third generation of mobile telephony, using its own Chinese technology. The UT Starcom technology was ideally suited to densely populated, smaller, poorer cities, and to mobile phone users who wanted a cheaper system which just allowed them to talk to each other. But eventually, the all-powerful Telecommunications Ministry, which controlled China Mobile, had its way. UT Starcom had to retreat, its telephony systems were closed down, and UT Starcom (which is still listed on NASDAQ) had to reinvent itself as a designer and manufacturer of telecoms software for global telecoms companies like Sprint.

If proof were needed of the all-pervading authority of the Chinese Government in the Chinese economy, the story of UT Starcom provided it. The company's technology provided poorer Chinese with effective mobile communications when the cost of a mobile system provided by market leaders Ericsson, Nokia or Motorola was unaffordable. In a country like the United States, consumers decide what they want to buy and use. There, it is the market which decides largely on which technologies succeed and which do not. But in China, the government played, and still plays a sometimes decisive role in deciding which companies can be successful. For a private company in China to survive and flourish, it has to prove it's a good Chinese citizen, from the Communist Party's perspective.

With my assistant Jim Sun, I had made a bet on China's internet companies. As we delved deeper into this sector, its exciting prospects became even more apparent. We heard of a private company which, starting in 1998, had developed an online system for individuals to book hotels and travel online, called Ctrip. When Ctrip sold its shares to the public in the middle of 2004, we met the management, and I interviewed one of its founders, a man called Neil Shen who had been a banker in Hong Kong with Deutsche Bank (and went on later to bring one of the most successful West Coast venture capital companies, Sequoia Capital, to China). Neil's experience was similar to mine at Sparkice, except that he and his colleagues had been successful in creating a functioning team with a software system which really worked. I understood what he had been through, and the excitement and satisfaction he felt at bringing his brainchild through its growing up pains to its coming out party. In the intervening years, Ctrip has become a staple in Chinese travellers' lives, and it continues today to provide a very useful public service. But severe competition within China from other service providers has eroded its profitability, and its share price has hardly changed in the fifteen or so years since its public listing.

Another Chinese start-up, which had started around the same time as Ctrip, provided online and mobile based games which were proving extremely popular with Chinese teenagers, as well as an online chat system which we thought would appeal strongly to the Chinese, with their close ties of family and friends. The company was called Tencent, and it sold its first shares to the public in Hong Kong in the middle of 2004 at a price about one-thousandth of its share price today.

Looking around me in Shanghai in 2003 and early 2004, I decided that China was on another growth spurt. The evidence was there, in front of my eyes: in the investments being made in construction, and in the optimism and confidence which I saw when I visited one or other of the private Chinese companies which we worked with. I started to think about the beneficiaries of the explosive expansion that I saw around me. Private companies were inactive in government controlled sectors, like telecoms or banking, and in sectors which required large amounts of capital, like construction and shipping. If I wanted to understand Chinese infrastructure and communications, I had to get closer to the state owned sector.

When I was advising a London based hedge fund some years earlier on their Chinese investment strategy, I had come across a Chinese steel company which had become famous in Mao's time as a model of China's centrally planned sector, and which had participated at an early stage in China's huge programme of privatisation. The company, called Ma'anshan (meaning Horse Hill) was based in Anhui province, about four hours by train from Shanghai. I sent them a message that I was a Western analyst based in Shanghai, and would like to visit them in order to report on their progress to the investors and banks in Europe and the United States who read our investment reports. I expected that this introduction would be attractive to Ma'anshan Steel, because as a company whose shares were listed on the Hong Kong stock exchange, they would wish to communicate with their investors in order to increase the value of their stock price. Steel companies had lost much of their appeal for investors as the appetite of developed countries for steel products had moderated. The industry had become highly competitive, and many steel companies based in the West had disappeared or merged. I was not disappointed. Ma'anshan replied quickly to my message saying that I was welcome, and asking when I would visit.

The following week, at about six o'clock in the morning I left my apartment in Puxi to take the underground to Shanghai South railway station. This was one of Shanghai's two enormous railway stations, rivalling New York's Grand Central Station in size. I weaved my way through the thousands of arriving, departing and waiting passengers to the large electronic signboard which displayed the trains with their numbers, departure times and destinations. Fortunately, I had reserved a seat, for by the time I had found my train and got on it, all twelve coaches were full. From Shanghai, the train ran ultimately to Wuhan, an important central city on the Yangtse several hundred miles from Shanghai, and it took a day and a night to get there. (Note: China's high-speed rail system has cut this journey to three hours.) Once the train started, as befitting its express status, it stopped only rarely. Ma'anshan was the fourth stop, and when I climbed down from the train, I was easily able to find a taxi to take me to the steel factory, already visible from the train station, and dominating the town.

Eventually I found myself in a meeting room sitting at a long table with the company secretary. He told me he had worked for Ma'anshan since his early twenties, thirty years ago. He described China's steel industry. China, he said, was at the beginning of a long period of economic expansion, during which the construction of buildings, bridges and all kinds of infrastructure would develop at a fast and sustained rate. This would place heavy demands on steel, obviously a key component of construction. He told me that Ma'anshan had always been known as the Chinese steel company which produced steel railway tracks, but it had started to expand its capacity in recent years by importing the machinery from Germany which it needed to manufacture steel girders, or H beams. Ma'anshan was now a leader in this sector, much in demand in China for every large built structure. He explained that deposits of iron ore, a key input into the steel manufacturing process, were limited in China, and only a few steel makers possessed their own supplies. The other Chinese steel factories had to import the raw material, mainly from Brazil and Australia, and India was also a smaller iron ore supplier. The limited availability of this vital raw material would push up the price of this essential input. This, he said, would favour companies like Ma'anshan who had their own supplies of the key raw material for making steel.

Another vital input to steelmaking, he continued, was electricity. Steel companies without their own iron ore might be able to stay competitive by having access to cheap electricity supplies. In China, this applied particularly to steel companies based near the hydroelectric projects based on the rivers which ran east and south from the Tibetan highlands into China. He projected that the non-availability of these two essential inputs, iron ore and power, would force many steel factories in China to disappear, and he added that this consolidation was in line with the Chinese Government's policy of shuttering smaller steel mills in order to create a smaller number of very large steel companies which would become China's national champions. He foresaw that Ma'anshan would be one of these favoured large companies, and that China's steel production would double from its then level of 200 million tonnes per annum. This projection made the outlook for Ma'anshan look very promising.

I was interested to hear this positive, expert view of the direction of China's economic travel, because it was in line with my own ideas, which contrasted strongly with the perceptions of most external observers of China in these early years of the millennium. It was also interesting to hear an insider's view of the future of the Chinese steel industry — expansion and consolidation, with the emergence, in his view, of a small number of very large Chinese steel mills, of which his own company Ma'anshan would be one. In fact, this outlook has come to pass, but it has taken a decade longer than the Ma'anshan director thought in 2004, and only because the Chinese Government started reduce to capacity significantly in 2015. Meanwhile, Ma'anshan has increased its annual steel output from 5 million tonnes when I visited the company, to 18 million tonnes today. His projection of 200 hundred million tonnes of Chinese steel output has been proved, in 2020, to be too small by a factor of about five times.

After our discussion, he took me on a tour of the steel factory, where I saw the huge steel furnace being upended to pour molten steel into the H-beam forms. When the time came to take my leave, the director shook my hand warmly, and told me that I was the first foreign financial analyst for several months to visit his factory. I promised him that I would send him a copy of my investment report. I felt I had made a friend. We returned to the railway station in a company car through streets which looked poor and polluted. Several hours later, we were back in Shanghai. Having written up my notes during the return journey to Shanghai, I was able to prepare and send out a positive report within a week or so. I'm glad to say that Ma'anshan's share price doubled in the following months as worldwide investors realised the new buoyancy of the Chinese economy.

At around the same time as my trip to Ma'anshan, I became interested in another Chinese state owned company which dominated river and coastal shipping around Shanghai, and which was beginning to become a force in international shipping as well. It seemed to me that China Shipping, for that was the company's name, controlled a part of the link between China's heartland, where hundreds of millions of hard-working Chinese worked twelve-hour shifts in export factories, and the developed world which was buying these products in ever larger quantities. Another interesting aspect of China Shipping was that it specialised in shipping oil. China was set, in my view, to rival the United States as the world's largest oil importer in the fairly near future. (This actually came to pass a few years ago.) After visiting Ma'anshan, I went to see China Shipping because, in addition to my interest in the company, I had learned that talking to Chinese companies about their business was a great way of finding out what was really going on inside China. The visit did not disappoint on either score, and I became even more optimistic about the prospects for China's economy over the next few years as a result.

The consequence of all these activities was that I had a grandstand micro-view of an event which was remarkable, if not unique in world history. China was waking up, and one-fifth of the world's population, for many centuries hidden behind a self-created wall of culture and language, had set out on the road of growth and integration with the rest of the planet. I saw, time and again, that the Chinese were superb businesspeople, whether they were working for a large state owned company or in an entrepreneurial venture. Somehow, they all had an instinctive understanding of trading and business. They all wanted to get ahead, and they had the work ethic and the imagination to succeed. But their political and cultural attitudes owed everything to Chinese history and culture, and were far removed from the West.

Very few people in the West seemed at this point to grasp what was going on in China, or seemed to appreciate what the global impact on the world of China's emergence was going to be. My friend James Kynge, who had learned Chinese at college in Britain before becoming a *Financial Times* journalist in China, addressed this huge mismatch in understanding and expectations in his 2005 book, *China Shakes the World*. The prize-winning success of James' book shows how surprised many people were to read about China's emergence and its future impact on their own lives. One way that I was able to exploit this gap, between reality on one side of the world, and mistaken perception on the other, is the subject of the next chapter.

Once again, I found myself living in China with my family six thousand miles away. But this time, I was elated, not depressed, at what I found around me. I wasn't the complete master of my destiny, because my wife and I were minority shareholders in the company we had created. But there was no way on our own that we could have started a bank, with all the operating licences, compliance and capital backing that was required. As it was, we had an appreciable interest in an entity that was already valuable, and would become more so as our business developed, and as China became more attractive. We were on an exciting ride into the future. Moreover, we had been profitable almost from the beginning of the venture, which gave us a large degree of comfort. If we needed to raise more capital, we could do so on good terms, and we didn't have to go begging.

IX

ASCENDING TO HEAVEN

To most people, hedge funds mean money — lots of it. Stories about hedge fund managers have become legend: buying the most expensive houses in London and New York, paying the largest financial settlements ever recorded in a divorce suit, owning the biggest yachts in the Mediterranean.

Earlier, I had spent some months helping some friends establish their hedge fund in London, so I had learned something about these fabled beasts. The early hedge fund starters had enjoyed an advantage of obscurity. At that time in the 1960s and 1970s, investment managers had not yet become the rock-stars of the financial world. On the contrary, then, and even in the 1980s, investment management was still a job often done by retired army majors and elderly accountants, for modest salaries only slightly better than their pensions.

But hedge funds changed all that. Emerging from a few specialist funds based in New York managed in the 1970s by highly skilled and experienced managers (like Jim Rogers, Julian Robertson and George Soros) for the ultra-rich, by the late 1980's, the breakneck expansion of the financial industry had encouraged their proliferation.

As hedge funds started to attract investment from pension funds and insurance companies, the available assets to be managed increased exponentially, and the industry grew by several times in a few years. Hedge funds changed from being a highly specialised product shared by a few very wealthy families, to the ultimate in get rich quick schemes for ambitious young entrepreneurs possessing a good line in self-promotion. The famous 'two-and-twenty' formula brought a fee every year of 2% charged on managed funds, plus 20% of the capital gains. A managed hedge fund of $500 million, a sum considered modest in this supercharged world, which gained 15% in a year would generate a total return to the fund manager of US$25 million. Increase the fund size, and with virtually no corresponding increase in costs, it's easy to see where the yachts, houses and divorce settlements come from.

The hedge fund industry attracts the prettiest girls and the best clothes, but also the best educations and the sharpest minds. Mediocrities know that it's better for them not to try and ascend to these Himalayan heights, where the air becomes rarefied. It was therefore with some foreboding that I set forth, early in 2004, on my mission to persuade the London investing world that China was not a 'sell', as it had been considered by most investors since the Asian financial crisis of 1997, but a 'buy'. I had formed my relatively optimistic view over the six months that I had been living in Shanghai. On my extensive travels around the Yangtse basin in search of prospective targets for our fundraising business, I had seen a few of the myriad fast-growing, highly volatile and uncertain private Chinese businesses which had sprung up like weeds following rain, as confidence seeped back into the Chinese economy. An important marker for this renewed confidence had been laid down a year earlier by a well-publicised, large investment from the doyen of professional investors, the American Warren Buffett, in China's largest state owned oil company. Although feelings in the rest of the world toward China were still depressed, on my travels in the Yangtse basin I could perceive a spring in the Chinese step. Extraordinarily, my banking competitors were still all based in Hong Kong, whose business temperature was at that time much closer to San Francisco, New York and London than it was to Shanghai and Beijing. The people in Hong Kong were all still stuck in the gloomy Western outlook toward China. As the only Western financial analyst based then in Shanghai — unbelievable, yet true — I believed I could see an opportunity.

Arriving in London after a long flight from Shanghai, my confidence was dented by the cool reception I received from my colleagues. They did not share my enthusiasm for a Chinese economic recovery, and treated my optimistic outpourings with reserve, even disdain. Didn't I know, they said, that China was being pumped up with money issued by the Chinese Government? In a few months, the whole inflated balloon would collapse, leaving me, and other similarly foolish optimists, looking sorry for ourselves. But I told myself that I must know more than they did, living as I did every day in the heart of the dragon, and not 6,000 miles away from it. So forth I went, visiting several investors in London's City district every day to tell them the good news.

But everywhere I went, my reception was very similar to the one I had already received from my London colleagues. One fund manager after another treated my idea that China was at the beginning of a historic growth period with polite scepticism. The meetings adopted a pattern. I would start by explaining my view that China was on a growth spurt: the Chinese Government was ramping up its public investment in infrastructure, and private companies were beginning to play a much larger role on the Chinese stage. At that point, investors would express their incredulity that private companies could operate successfully in China, which everyone knew was dominated by large, government owned companies. As few of these privately owned Chinese companies were large enough, at this point, to have made any impression on the Chinese economy, or on the financial markets, and those that had could show only short track records, it was hard for me to point to specific successful examples which could support my case. Then, the rises in the prices of basic building commodities, like copper and steel, which to me were clear evidence of a sharp revival in business sentiment, were dismissed by my audience as mere expressions of a surge in liquidity, and no more. When the liquidity disappeared, they said, commodity prices would slump back to their levels of the last decade or so. Finally, alarm was expressed at the pile of debt which the Chinese Government's investment was creating. How was this debt to be repaid? After an hour or so of gloom, I left for the next meeting, incredulous that so many people could be wrong, and not fundamentally altered in my view that China was at the beginning of something remarkable and surprising.

One of my final meetings was with a young man (let us call him George) who had recently joined a small team based in Mayfair, London. With his business partner, he had left his safe, well-paid job at a large, prestigious investment management house to try his luck with a small hedge fund. As I told my story, I started to feel, at last, that here was a receptive audience. I had found someone who was looking for a way to be different to the crowd, to place a large bet which would turn up trumps. In our first meeting, George played devil's advocate for a while, stating that the three separate investment consultants employed by the hedge fund were each of the view that China was going through something of a bubble. Their advice was to sell that market, not to buy it. But he did not completely dismiss my ideas. I felt that, maybe, here was someone who I could work with.

Sure enough, a couple of weeks later George called me, to say he was coming round to our office in Cornhill, opposite the Bank of England, to talk to me. Once we were seated in our small conference room, he told me that since my visit, he had been doing intensive research, and the signs were, from what he had seen and read, that I was right, that China was on a roll. George said that he had never been to China, and would like to go there, accompanied by me. This news caused a stir in my office, because until then, I had not been able to find anyone in the City of London to agree with or support my optimistic view on China. But one of my colleagues knew of George as an exceptionally intelligent and hard-working individual. She was impressed by his positive conclusion, and that helped me to persuade some of my colleagues that I might be right.

A few weeks later, I found myself flying from London back to Shanghai, me sitting at the back of the plane, and my young friend George at the front, in first-class. Hedge fund managers never fly anything else but first-class, but our young China banking business was still losing money, and I didn't feel up to spending the extra few thousand dollars to join him. The airport we touched down at was brand new, located in rice fields far into Pudong, the development zone identified by the Shanghai Government in 1991 when the Chinese leader Deng Xiaoping and Beijing had given the green light to Shanghai to go ahead with its development. Today, Pudong Airport is surrounded by busy streets, high-rise office buildings and apartment blocks, and it reached its planned throughput capacity some years ago. Then, however, only almost twenty years ago, it seemed like something from the movie *Independence Day*, a huge visitor from another planet, plonked down in the middle of a timeless Chinese peasant scene.

As we drove in our S-class Mercedes limo from the airport to our hotel, I regaled George with stories from my time living in Shanghai nearly a decade earlier, while he stared out of the car window at the high-rise cranes and construction sites which we drove past, one after another. I had chosen the new Hyatt Hotel to stay in because I knew that George could not fail to be impressed by his journey in an elevator straight to the forty-eighth floor, at high speed. Here, from the hotel reception on top of the tallest building in Shanghai, one had a magnificent view of the Huangpu River with the famous Shanghai Bund beyond, and on the other side, high-rise cranes stretching away into a haze of pollution.

Our first visit was to our office, located in the same building, about twenty floors below our hotel. As we entered the small office with its magnificent view, George hurried over to our office computer to check the markets. He returned with a smile on his face. He told me that a few days before our trip, using the capital in his fund, plus some borrowing, he had acquired about five per cent of the stock of a major copper producer. This gave his fund raw exposure to the volatile price of a vital commodity used in building infrastructure. This was a major investment of tens of millions of dollars, requiring a substantial part of his fund. He had bet a large part of the farm on what he had heard from me and on his subsequent research. He told me that the price of the shares had already risen since his purchase by nearly 30%, and his bet was already looking very good. For the rest of the week-long Chinese trip, a grin was never far from his face.

From there, we went to see a local state owned Shanghainese company which dominated the coastal and Yangtse River shipping trade. This was one important part of the evidence I wanted to provide George, of a forthcoming boom in Chinese business activity, because a river and coastal shipper, which moves food, oil and manufactured products up and down the Yangtse River and the Chinese coast is a good barometer of trade. The business manager whom we met at the company did not disappoint me. Neither did the others at the various Shanghai based companies which we went to see over the next couple of days, mostly state owned, which were involved in a wide range of activities, from producing and selling milk and beer to manufacturing high specification electrical transformers. I remember, in particular, when we visited the largest Shanghai-based commercial bank, George's surprise at the high levels of profitability which the bank enjoyed — much higher, he explained, that any comparable bank in North America or Europe. I was able to respond, by way of explanation, that these large Chinese Government owned banks were able to keep the interest rates which they paid their depositors very low because the banks formed a critical means of support for the government owned corporations which controlled the sinews of the economy — banking, telephone, water and electricity, real estate and so on. The bank's depositors, many of whom were Chinese families, were happy to entrust their savings to a 'good cause' (in other words, the wellbeing of the Chinese state), and to give up some interest on their money in return for the complete security provided by a bank owned and operated by the Chinese Government.

Once again, I learned how hard it was to explain the unique Chinese economic system to an outsider, even though, in this case, the outsider, George, was a top economics graduate from Oxford University and had more than ten years' experience as a money manager. Like his colleagues, he came from a Western system which aspired to a competitive marketplace, which in turn provided the average person with the best possible service and lowest possible prices, which the collapse of the Soviet Communist system fifteen years earlier had confirmed to be the best and only system. How could an economic system work in which the main player, controlling the rules and many of the important economic inputs, was a government controlled by a Communist Party which, nominally at least, still thought Lenin had it right? I recalled to George the metaphor used by a leading Chinese theoretician and economic planner from the early Reform period in the late 1970s and early '80s, Chen Yun. He saw the Chinese economy (and society) like a bird inside a cage. The bird was the market system; the cage was the set of rules that the party created around the market. In those early 'noughty' days, when the Chinese economy was taking off after the Asian crisis like a moon rocket, the cage and bird metaphor seemed out of date. Today, however, we can see that it is not.

From Shanghai, George and I flew to Beijing, where we stayed in another beautiful hotel located on Jianguomen street, quite near to the Forbidden City and to Tienanmen Square, two places next to each other at the centre of the city. There we visited several more companies, including the principal Beijing power utility, which had sold some of its shares to the investing public in Hong Kong, demonstrating again the ingenious way in which the Chinese Government made use of stock markets, normally associated with capitalism in its rawest form, to further their growth objectives by raising external capital and increasing transparency, while at the same time maintaining control of all the important Chinese economic actors like electricity generation.

On the last evening of our trip, I arranged a dinner between George and China's leading reform-oriented economist, whom I had known since he studied for his doctorate at Oxford in the late 1980s. Swapping Oxford anecdotes gave George confidence in my economist friend's judgement, and when the Chinese economist said that he believed that China's growth really was taking off, the crowning moment to our visit arrived. By now the price of the copper company shares which George had bought a couple of weeks earlier had increased by a further 20%. It really did seem as if George had captured the moment of which investors dream: owning a stock which everyone else wanted to buy.

This short trip with George gave me a lot more confidence in China's recovery from the harsh winter of the Asian economic crisis. It was like early spring in the economy of a large country. Growth was everywhere, much of it uncontrolled. The tall building cranes which had been lying idle for years in Shanghai were moving again. Every day, buildings soared into the sky, with electrical welding torches flashing their neon signatures around the clock. This miracle was made possible by the many millions of male Chinese peasant farmers who arrived in Shanghai every year to become building workers, from small rural villages and towns in the centre and west of the country. Leaving their wives and children at home, after Chinese New Year, they travelled on slow trains to the big cities of the east, where they could earn twenty or fifty times more, living (if they were lucky) in large dormitories built by their employer. Often they were to be seen walking along girders hundreds of feet up in the air, without any means of support, Death-rates were high, and violent episodes arising from non-payment of their wages at the end of the month or quarter were not uncommon. But the work got done, and the buildings, one after another, rose high into the sky in astonishingly short periods of time. About two years to construct a 50-storey office building, including its foundations, seemed to be the norm.

This was the beginning of the China boom which has changed our world. At this time, though, most Westerners didn't know about it, or if they had heard about it, most disbelieved it. The idea of China becoming rich and powerful sparked some kind of cognitive dissonance in many Western minds, particularly American ones. Was it a hangover from the Asian crisis in the late 1990s which had seen 'successful' Asian tiger economies like Thailand, Indonesia and South Korea go spectacularly bankrupt? Or was it because the West was scared of a rich and powerful China?

I didn't care what the reason was, because I knew that I was like the one-eyed man in the kingdom of the blind: I could see something that most others could not. George's copper investment just went up and up. He sold a few years later, after he had made a profit of about six times his initial investment, then realised he had made a mistake, bought back in, and sold out finally after a further gain of more than 50% — a profit since starting of about ten times, over a period of about four years. Fortune favours the brave, and George, and his hedge fund company, became very rich and famous in the dog-eat-dog world of hedge funds.

It took a few months for the investing world to start changing its mind about China. But gradually the banking offices in Beijing and Shanghai, which had all been closed in 1997 and 1998 as the Asian crisis hit, were reopened, and a new generation of 'China experts' started to appear on financial television shows on Bloomberg and CNBC. When we opened our office in Shanghai in 2003, the building was 60% empty; two years later, it was full, often with the offices of our competitors.

After I had been in Shanghai for a couple of months, I moved my accommodation from a slightly rundown apartment block near the Hilton Hotel in central Shanghai, to a new residential project in Pudong which lay within walking distance of my office. The just completed development contained several large apartment buildings, each of which contained dozens of two- and three-bedroom apartments. There was a swimming pool, and two restaurants, one providing Chinese food and the other European. I rented a two-bed apartment, at a lower price than I had been paying previously, from a Malaysian Chinese who had bought the apartment during the pre-build marketing, at a discount, and who was keen to get the apartment working. I discovered that all the hundreds of apartments in the development belonged to Chinese families, most of whom lived outside China, in Singapore, Hong Kong, Indonesia or Malaysia, but who all believed in China's economic ascent and were brave and shrewd enough to invest in line with their conviction for a prosperous Chinese future. How right they were.

My children, then both at boarding school in England, flew from London to Shanghai during their summer holidays to spend a few days with me. During the daytime, I left them in the apartment doing their holiday homework, or watching television, and took them out in the evening to see the Shanghai sights and visit seafood restaurants. After a week of this, they were taken away by my Chinese brother-in-law to spend a few days visiting a famous mountain in the centre of China, then flew back to Chicago with him to spend the rest of the summer holiday in his house, playing with his two children in his swimming pool.

I realised that, once again, my family responsibilities were conflicting with my work. Living and working in Shanghai at that time, I knew I was in the epicentre of a historic moment in Chinese and in world history. China's emergence was happening all around me. I saw it every day. But my children aged every day too, and soon they would be becoming young adults. I decided to return to London so I could spend much more time seeing them grow up. Within a month, I had terminated the lease on my apartment in Pudong, and handed over my responsibilities as research director in Shanghai to a Chinese speaking American accountant who had joined our research team.

***

The building in London's financial district which housed our London office was more than one hundred years old. Our company's expansion, in particular the requirement to separate our ten-man trading and settlement floor from the fast-growing team which processed our capital raising activities for Chinese companies in London and Hong Kong, strained our interior designers' ingenuity, and the office was starting to bulge at the seams. But I was able to find a small office at the back of the building, where I could gain enough quiet and privacy to continue producing China research notes.

By now, the sounds from the drum we had been beating for a few months about China's return to fast economic growth had reverberated beyond London. Our burgeoning investor client base now stretched to Paris, Geneva, Zurich, Frankfurt, Amsterdam, Brussels, Stockholm, Milan, New York and San Francisco. Equally, our fame in China had also spread, assisted and supported greatly by the partnership we maintained with our banking partners in Shanghai. Soon we learned that our Chinese partners were establishing an office in Hong Kong, to better serve their Chinese clients. We realised that this development could undercut our partners' support for our efforts in Hong Kong. However, as China grew, their commercial activities, both private and state owned, increasingly needed a global audience and market to grow into. Our Western connections and capabilities continued to be a significant complement to our Chinese partners' activities on the mainland of China. Given the sharp division between Chinese cultural norms and Western ones, I believed it would be years, decades even, before our Chinese partners were able to match and challenge our London based marketing and capital raising capabilities.

At this time, a few years after the millennium and a couple of years before the great financial crisis, London, and its financial district (their interests closely interrelated) were booming. The financial district (known as 'the City') was almost unrecognisable from the dirty, smoky streets which I, and a few others, could remember twenty-five years earlier, when some brokers used to still wear the top hats of years long past. These top hat wearers in fact belonged to a special fraternity: a small private partnership which had conducted Britain's national borrowing activities on the London market for two hundred years. It still did when I started work in the City, hence the top hats. The firm had only twelve partners. To become a partner meant usually that you had attended one of the leading English private schools (probably Eton), and Oxford or Cambridge (either would do), unless you were a mathematical genius, and could calculate changes in bond yields using pen, slide rule and paper within a few seconds. If you could, then you would be needed in the partners' meeting-room. In either case — mathematical competence or the 'right' background — a partnership at the firm was a ticket to riches. But in those far-off and very different days, it was considered very poor form to mention the fact of the riches, and no one in this, or similar City offices, ever discussed personal wealth or property. The then occupant of the position at the firm officially described as 'the Government Broker' had served as a very young man in a distinguished British Army regiment during the Second World War, and was famous in the City for being very deaf as a consequence. According to an apocryphal story, when he was told at lunch by his neighbour at the table, the senior partner of the firm, that there was a 'case of syphilis' in the firm, he had replied enthusiastically that it was good news, because he was getting tired of the French Beaujolais wine that the partners had been drinking recently with their lunch. The top hats only ended when, exactly two hundred years after the brokerage house had been established by British Prime Minister William Pitt (the Younger), the twelve-man private partnership allowed itself to be subsumed into a much larger banking organisation, one which had been started after World War Two by a brilliant Jewish financier who had escaped from Nazi Germany. Only a few years earlier, a City of London merger between Jews and Gentiles would have been unthinkable.

I remembered, too, the Stock Exchange building, completed in the 1970s, on whose large floor all trading in stocks, bonds and other financial instruments was conducted. Now, the space had been re-engineered into offices and restaurants. Small, hole-in-the-wall restaurants were still part of the City scene in those far off days, where before work you could sit down to a delicious greasy English breakfast washed down with strong cups of tea, and at lunch you could drink your way, with a friend or two, through a bottle of Chablis, over some potted shrimps. Getting to work was a fight through a packed underground train, in which nearly everyone had a cigarette hanging out of their mouth.

No, times had certainly changed, the City of London was on a pre-financial crisis roll, and we were a small part of it. British nationalities predominated in our small firm, numbering between forty and fifty, but we could also boast of others: some Chinese professionals, of course; an Indian, an American, a French woman, a Spanish computer expert, and so on. This was no more than a sign of the times. Every year, for the City then, was better than the one before. It is only in hindsight that we see now how close to the precipice of the great financial crash of 2007 and 2008 we were treading, at that time.

As our China banking venture prospered, we had started taking Chinese visitors to events in London, like the opera at Covent Garden. One guest was a Chinese girl in her thirties, who had co-founded one of the most successful online Chinese companies, which was about to be listed as a public company on the American exchange NASDAQ. She was visiting London with some of her colleagues to introduce her company to London based investors, and our company was showing her round. When I met her outside the opera house after her day of visits conducted by two of my younger colleagues, I noticed that she was wearing a diamond ring (from Tiffany in New York, she told us), and a fur coat, also from New York. What a contrast, I thought, to the downtrodden, blue-uniformed Chinese people who I had met on my first trip to China in the late 1980s.

Another opera guest was the chairman of our Chinese partner bank in Shanghai. He was a middle-aged, well-dressed man, who didn't speak much or any English, and can't have understood much of what was going on, but seemed to enjoy being in London's Royal Opera House: one of the temples of fashionable European society, if not culture. These visitors were the early forerunners of today's waves of well-heeled, very high-end Chinese tourist, the ones you see in Harrods in Knightsbridge, London, in Bloomingdales on Fifth Avenue, New York, and in the Hermès store in Faubourg Saint-Honoré in Paris.

The sweet smell of success had spread from our office along the street, and it had reached the office of our London banking partner. They were still much larger than us. But we were starting to catch up, in numbers of personnel and in revenues. Strong common interests still overrode the frictions and jealousies which threatened to develop between our organisation, the fast-growing Chinese subsidiary, and the parent. They, of course had a major interest in our success. If at some future point we capitalised the value of our business, perhaps via a sale of shares to the investing public, or perhaps through a direct sale of our business to another bank who wanted to gain access to China, then the shareholders of our banking partner, which owned the majority of our share capital, would be the largest beneficiary. The people who ran our London partner's business — the rugby player, the accountant and the hitman — were microscopically small shareholders, themselves, in our majority shareholder. Their financial rewards came largely through their annual salary, and in particular, their end of year bonuses, an essential part of any senior banker's compensation package. What our senior colleagues up the road wanted in particular from us was more Chinese business which we could share with them, especially London capital-raisings, which their organisation participated in, and whose substantial fees contributed to their end of year bonuses.

As our business developed, we considered amongst ourselves how our business strategy should evolve. One option was to continue as we were: locating companies within China, and then introducing them to the Western world which, at that time, was where the money was, and often where the markets for Chinese manufactured products were too. This strategy focused our revenue largely on activities which took place in London or in Hong Kong, outside of the Chinese mainland. News of success in raising capital in London had spread, and more Chinese companies were now looking to 'touch the golden dragon' as they put it. They ranged from successful, well-established private Chinese businesses, with three or four year profit track records, solid accounting systems and reputable managers, to highly speculative ventures, sometimes advertised as 'the next big thing in China', with little or no capital and no accounting systems. Fraud was a major threat. After all, this was a country at an early modern stage of financial development, which thirty years before had been a communist autarky. Where systems, processes and expectations existed, they were usually of Chinese origin and constructed to meet the lower expectations of a Chinese investing public. Creating strong corporate governance systems was an important part of our work. Then, some of the good, sound projects went to competitors, while the projects we declined as unreliable, or possibly fraudulent, were often able to find another bank eager for the banking fees, but without any of the experience or on the ground investigative resources that we had in place.

Chinese corporate demand for capital was growing strongly, but competition in the niche market we had developed was also becoming stronger. Maybe, we thought, we should build on our special advantage of familiarity with and strong connections inside the Chinese mainland. Ying, our CEO, with her strong understanding of and links to China, thought that we should expand onto the mainland itself. This was a time when the business of capital raising and financial advice in China was booming and proliferating. We knew there were a number of resident Chinese investment banks which covered their domestic market. Our Chinese partner, based in Shanghai, was one. But a successful, on the ground, mainland business would complement our existing offshore activities, and would also give us access to growing and potentially enormous revenue streams from companies within China.

I should emphasise the importance of Ying's contribution to the success of our Chinese banking venture. Her early experiences in China before and during the Cultural Revolution, as a young gymnast, then as a Red Guard and peasant worker on the fields, and finally as speechwriter for an important government organisation in Beijing gave her an unparalleled understanding of Chinese psychology and society. Over the years since leaving China, she had added a great deal of experience of deal-making between Western corporations and Chinese ones, and she had spent several years working in the financial services industry as a banker and stockbroker, in London, Beijing and Hong Kong. With her natural drive, intelligence and personal charisma, these experiences gave her a formidable set of advantages which enabled her to command the confidence of our rapidly expanding team, our partners and our clients, whether Chinese, European or American.

But her strategic approach was contentious, and not everyone supported it. A common reaction was: "If it's not broken, why fix it?" Why put new resources into a new strategy if the current one is working? The counterargument to this was that our existing business was becoming increasingly competitive, with some much larger, international Western banks starting to compete for Chinese business offshore. A move into mainland China would provide an enormous growth opportunity. In essence, the choice lay between a more modest, proven and smaller future, versus a potentially much larger opportunity which came with the risks of operating within mainland China.

Our London banking partners were not very enthusiastic about our ideas for development on the mainland of China. I think this was because they were enjoying the benefits from the current, offshore focused operation. They put less weight on long-term growth, and more weight on perceived risk, than we did, and they liked in particular the stream of London capital-raising transactions which we were bringing to the market, and to them. We decided, however that a mainland operating approach could be conducted in parallel with our existing operation, and we realised that we may have to consider pursuing this new strategic path with greater independence from our parent. We had already conducted successfully one fundraising exercise, on attractive financial terms, to boost our headcount and operating capability, and now had several City institutions as small investors in our business. We believed that we could do another such exercise, on a larger scale. We started to search for an investor, perhaps another financial services company, which could share our ideas, and join us as a financial partner to bring the idea to fruition. Our search took us around the City, and we held discussions with several possible partners. The success we had had in the previous financing round, and our operating profitability in a new, high-growth market led us to demand a high valuation on our capital. This ambitious valuation proved a hurdle to closing a deal.

Then someone suggested Japan. We knew that Japanese financial institutions were anxious to penetrate the still young Chinese market, as their industrial and high-tech companies had already done. As a service industry, however, which depended as much on relationships and perceptions as on products and price, Japanese banks suffered from the complex, often difficult relationship between Japan and China. The essential components of this relationship go back in history more than a thousand years, to the time when the Japanese started to copy and import Chinese culture, literature and methods of governance. The ancient Japanese imperial city of Kyoto was set out to lie north-south, in imitation of China's then imperial city Chang'an. Although the Japanese language sounds and is different to Chinese, written Japanese is based on the Chinese character system. Japan has an idiosyncratic and unique society, but nevertheless, China and Japan are tied together closely with bonds of shared culture. Yet, there are also real tensions between the two peoples, arising on the Chinese side from the Japanese invasion of China in the 1930s, and on the Japanese side by perceptions of the Chinese as a backward, inferior people. It is difficult for Japanese companies to operate successfully in China, although they clearly see the market's potential, they understand the kinds of products and services that Chinese people want, and they know how to go about marketing them. For that reason, we thought that it might be possible to present our London based, China-focused bank as a suitable intermediary, or as a route to China for a Japanese financial services institution which saw China as an expansion opportunity.

Fortunately, we were able to locate a highly experienced and expert intermediary in London, a British banker who had spent over a decade living in Tokyo as the representative of a major British bank. We knew that he had extensive contacts at high levels in the Japanese financial system. He agreed to help us. Within a few weeks, he was on a plane to Tokyo with my wife Ying, who was still the chief executive of our operation. He was able to arrange for her to spend several hours with the chief executive and senior managers of a major Japanese financial services company which saw China as an important market and were already looking for ways to access this opportunity. Finally, the Japanese asked her how much we wanted for an investment of new capital which would comprise a large minority stake in our business, of about 30%. The number mentioned by her was slightly above the high valuation which earlier had proved a stumbling block in London. But here in Japan, the valuation was not an obstacle. We had a deal.

Never had a thirty-six hour round trip, from London to Tokyo and back, turned out to be so rewarding.

X

WHAT IT MEANT, AND WHERE IT'S GOING

Within a few months, Ying and I had left. Our partners did not agree with the new strategy, and did not support it. As the parent company, which they led, owned more than half the shares in the company we had started together, it was us, not them, who had to go. A year or so later, the financial crisis struck, and a few months after that, the company was acquired by a Hong Kong based investing institution. That was the end of our Chinese business adventure. Fortunately, we had been able earlier to sell some of our shares at the much higher price which was obtainable before the financial crash. Ying went on to work for a large and successful hedge fund, and I turned to writing my first book, *China and the Credit Crisis: the emergence of a new world order*.

Hindsight is often ridiculed, but it has its uses. Looking back, what did I learn from almost two decades of close involvement with China during its early reawakening?

First, about business, and being an entrepreneur: 'Be careful who you get into bed with' applies just as much to business relationships as it does to personal relationships. The Chinese have an apt expression to describe a joint venture between a Chinese and a foreign company: one bed, two dreams. It applies equally to any business organisation. Individual motives differ, sometimes radically. However capable people are, or however affable they might appear to be, it's their underlying motivation which, in the end, drives what they do. The underlying motives of founders and key staff become very important as a successful business grows from a start-up to a substantial organisation employing many people. In the two businesses described in this book, both involved partners. In the first case, the failure of the partnership, due to differing underlying motives, turned out to be the critical factor which undermined the business. In the second, although the partnership was not problem free, it played a much more constructive role because the motives were better aligned. Working out motives is important. Sometimes these motives will be prima facie — of which the desire to make money is the commonest and most straightforward. But sometimes there's another buried motive which may come to light later, often when key decisions are being taken which affect the long-term future of the enterprise.

Unfortunately, it's difficult to recognise motives on first acquaintance with someone, especially if the person has a motive which they wish to conceal. What I learned is that it's important to be open-eyed and very clear-headed about business partners, especially when they are bringing an investment in your business whose desirability may make you inclined to overlook their personal characteristics.

Working between cultures, as we did between Western societies and China, exposes one to cross-cultural misunderstandings, which magnify enormously the chances of misunderstanding. Ying's role here was crucial, because her early experience in China, especially through the decade of the Cultural Revolution, allowed her to understand perfectly the background and motives of each and every Chinese person that we dealt with. At the same time, she had spent long enough in the West, married to a Englishman, to be able to comprehend the Western perspective. Ying's example shows how important it is not just to speak other countries' languages, but to be able to understand what different people are thinking about, and what is important to them, whether it be money, honour, status, friendship or something else.

What about integrity? Being honest and straightforward is a big advantage, but in my experience, especially where substantial amounts of money are involved, simple integrity is not as common as one might like it to be. It's a fact — sad or not — that I had more trouble with lack of integrity in the West than I did with my Chinese clients and employees. My experience was that once the Chinese agreed to something, they stuck to it. Readers should certainly not believe that Chinese people are inherently less trustworthy than Westerners. Beyond that, generalisations are not useful. Some people say that they will only deal with people who clearly have integrity; but restricting oneself just to dealing with that quite rare breed is a severe limitation. More realistically, I think one should value integrity highly, be aware when it may be missing, and take the necessary precautions.

The big point about all this is that, in business, people are easily the most important single factor, whether they be customers, suppliers, partners, employees, bosses or regulators. This fact is very helpful in China, because it's a people and relationship oriented society, where good personal relationships can make the difference between getting and not getting approval or a licence, or between making or not making a sale. Some businesses depend on one person, so with these, being able to understand and deal with people is not so important. For example, Bill Gates' core skill was writing computer programmes. He co-wrote the computer code for IBM's pioneering personal computer which provided the platform for Microsoft's success, and he also masterminded and wrote much of the code for Microsoft's flagship product Windows. After his co-founder left early, Gates controlled the business. Essentially, especially in the first two decades when the business was growing fast and building, he needed people around him who did what he told them to do. Steve Ballmer was one of them.

Companies like Microsoft are the exception. Most businesses are not dominated by one person. They succeed because of interactions between people with different talents, who work together in a productive and reasonably harmonious way. Collecting and keeping those people together is a key skill and a core success factor. Identifying and training talent as a means of maintaining and building the enterprise is a skill that separates many outstanding leaders from the others. (Here, I salute the pioneering work of my friend and former colleague Professor Sydney Finkelstein at Dartmouth College in America, who has written about these kinds of leaders in his book, *Superbosses*.)

Something else I found out, from my experience, is that most people in the West have a soft spot for an entrepreneur, and they try to be helpful and go the extra mile as a result. Maybe that's because many people working in large Western organisations have an entrepreneur inside them, trying to get out. In China, though, it's a little different, because there, 'entrepreneur' means 'outside the system', and it's the system in China, with the Communist Party at its core, that represents stability and even national identity to many Chinese. Chinese entrepreneurs have to find ways of getting inside the system, in order to obtain licences and get bank loans, for example. The fact that Chinese entrepreneurs have to persuade government officials to help them often means that money passes hands, from the entrepreneur to the official. This could be in the form of cash, or it could also be in the form of part-ownership of a holding company based in a jurisdiction like the British Virgin Islands which protects corporate identities, making it almost impossible for anyone to discover who the beneficial owners of a company. As a consequence, in China, entrepreneurs are often associated by the general public with corruption. That doesn't stop the extremely enterprising Chinese people from being entrepreneurs, but it can make life difficult for them, especially under a regime like the current one which uses anti-corruption laws as an important means of gaining popular support from Chinese people (as well as neutralising its enemies). Traditionally, Chinese people feel obliged to treat foreigners very politely, and this courtesy often overrides any suspicion they might have of foreign entrepreneurs. I certainly benefited from this attractive national characteristic.

They say that persistence is everything, and I think that's true. You probably learn more from failure than you do from success; if so, failure provides a good platform for starting again, and doing better. Certainly, the lessons I learned from our first business, about the importance of a clear, simple plan, cashflow and above all, having a solid partner were useful later. Another important point I learned about is hubris: if you think you're near the top of the mountain, then you're only part of the way up, with the peak obscured by a false crest. Many businesses, some of them large and old ones, have come to grief as a result of hubris, or thinking they are at the top. Conversely, one reason for the success of Bill Gates was that he reminded himself constantly that, if everything went wrong, Microsoft was only twelve months away from bankruptcy.

That was probably an exaggeration, but as an entrepreneur, it was a useful habit to have. There were moments when I thought, for a moment or two, that we had done it, and we were at the top. In a business which is striking out a new path, it's sometimes easy to think like that, when a couple of things go well. But it's always a mistake, because you're never at, or probably even near the top of the mountain, and you're never done.

Then, about China. It's a huge, ancient country which, I learned, in its fundamentals, owes absolutely nothing to the West, and which has a structural, underlying tendency toward dictatorship. When Portugal and Spain became the first European colonial powers in the 1500s, China was already well past the peak of its civilisation, having invented many things which, passing west along the Silk Road, became staples of European civilisation. Chinese society is 'sui generis' — of itself — and the two core influences of Daoism and Confucianism can still be seen clearly in the way the Chinese people think and behave towards others. With Daoism comes the idea of balance, compromise and consensus, that everything has its opposing partner, which it depends on to make a whole. Without white, there is no black; without strong there is no weak; and without man, there is no woman. There is a natural order, and we humans are part of it. With Confucianism comes the idea of man-made order and ritual, and the key social conventions of Chinese life: respect for elders, the family and tradition, benevolence, humility, duty, honesty. Even the most fleeting consideration of this ancient, rich Chinese heritage gives rise to the realisation that our Western code of behaviour, drawn from Greek philosophy and Christian morality, topped off with Adam Smith ideas of freedom, bears little resemblance to the Chinese tradition.

China is a uniquely homogeneous large country, with 95% of its huge population belonging to the same ethnic group, the Han. (Compare that to the extraordinary racial diversity of the other superpower, America.) This ethnic and cultural homogeneity means that the Chinese people regard themselves as a separate ethnic unit, and they think of togetherness as their natural state. They regard national unity and wholeness as a good and healthy thing. But to achieve this unified state in a huge country containing much variation from north to south, and east to west, experience has taught the Chinese that a strong centralised system is necessary. That is why China has been ruled for most of the last two thousand years by one person, usually (but not always) a man. Dictatorship remains today the essential flaw of traditional Chinese governance, because the Chinese people, being themselves very practical and non-ideological, see strong, centralised rule as the only way to avoid the dreaded chaos and destruction which has followed in the past from a disunited China. History shows that strong, centralised rule often drifts into dictatorship.

We in the West consider personal freedom — of thought, speech, choice and action, within the law — as the ultimate goal of our society. We have developed systems of governance and law which support that freedom. The Chinese idea of freedom is constrained, by their circumstances, to the means to prosper, and to exist unmolested, within the family system. For most Chinese, unlimited freedom, of the Western kind, is unthinkable, and even undesirable because it could imply a world in which the familiar Chinese state no longer exists — and what would happen then?

The most important thing I have learned about China is that it is fundamentally different, and will remain different, because it will remain China. To the Chinese, the country's evolution since 1980 has been 'opening up'; but to many Westerners, it has been 'becoming more like us'.

But the Western idea, born in the 1970s from the meeting of President Nixon with the Chinese leader Mao, that over time China will become more Western and 'more like us' has never really been on the cards, for a single moment. How could we in the West believe that China could become Westernised? We wanted to believe that, because the commercial opportunities from China's opening-up were so attractive and potentially game-changing. Clearly, also, it seemed that having China inside a Western tent was better than having it outside, especially while Soviet Russia existed. Furthermore, we thought that the Western system based on the idea of personal freedom could be the only human system of organisation and governance which could work. This idea was underlined by the termination of the Soviet Communist system, and it received formal recognition in 1992 when the book, *The End of History and the Last Man* by Francis Fukuyama, was published. In his now famous book, Fukuyama claimed that freedom and equality were universal, and were not constrained by the Christian and Greek traditions which had produced Western democracy. Fukuyama's doctrine meant that there was nothing to stop China from becoming like the West — even, in terms of personal freedom, from becoming like America. But my two decades of close personal involvement with China and its people have taught me that this is not the case, and can never be the case, because the Chinese tradition (about which I think that Fukuyama knows little) is fundamentally different to the Western one and is deeply rooted.

In the Chinese system, law has a different meaning. Laws do not exist in China to protect the freedoms of individuals, but to permit the functioning of society in an orderly way, whether from a commercial or from a social perspective. Human beings do not possess the inalienable, extensive rights in China that they do in the West. That fact explains the development in China of the family as the core social unit, because in a society in which individuals receive little or no legal protection, some kind of social unit becomes essential, and Confucianism has determined that this unit is the family, with the matriarch at its centre. In China, 'laws' mean 'rules', except in the commercial world, where Western ideas of equity and fairness before the law have gained traction as China's economy has become more interdependent with the rest of the world.

All this means that Chinese people are influenced in different ways than Westerners are. In a system lacking laws which protect the rights of the individual, personal honour and reputation is fundamental to a Chinese, because his (or her) existence depends on the way that others think about and treat him, and also because he is part of a family system that may stretch sideways to many distant cousins, and back into time for hundreds of years. Direct descendants of Confucius, the members of the Kong family, describe themselves as number 67 or number 72: meaning that they belong to the 67th or 72nd generation of direct descent from Kong Fu Shi, who lived about 500 years BC. The Kong family take ancestor worship to an extreme extent, but most Chinese families know of and honour their ancestors of at least several generations back. An insult to them as individuals is also an insult to former generations.

The other side of this coin is that Chinese allow personal sentiments to govern their personal relationships, and often these personal sentiments will outweigh other considerations, be they political or commercial. When a Chinese feels that he has been treated with the courtesy appropriate to his position, then he feels obliged to respond in kind; and when he feels he has been treated with warmth and kindness, then he will respond in kind as well. Many Westerners also like to be treated politely and warmly, and these factors are not unique to the Chinese. But in China they determine the nature and outcome of a relationship, whereas in New York or London, personal likes and dislikes can be set aside, as many people socialise and do business with others that they may not like or esteem.

In China, once one becomes aware of and familiar with these important characteristics, I found that they actually make relationships more delicate and nuanced affairs, because both sides place great store by them. One's enjoyment of personal relationships is heightened.

If China is going to stay Chinese, and not become Westernised, what does that mean? China's natural slant towards centralisation and strong leadership (verging on dictatorship) means that the main issue for the next few years will be China's system of governance, and in particular, the position of President Xi Jinping and the role of the Communist Party.

It is well known that since 2015, President Xi has shifted his own and the party's position very substantially away from consensus style leadership and a mixed socialist economy, towards personal dictatorship, and in the economy, state capitalism dominated by government owned and government controlled companies This has alarmed many, because Deng Xiaoping's big takeaway from the period of Mao's rule, and in particular the Cultural Revolution, was that the Chinese leadership must be limited in order to stop Mao's kind of highly toxic one-man dictatorship from destroying the country ever again. A two-term limit, each term of five years, was placed on the president's term in office. Many Chinese regarded this presidential term limit as a very significant step away from the traditional Chinese drift toward dictatorship, towards some kind of consensual or more liberal system of governance.

But in 2017, President Xi ended this two-term limit on the presidential term of office, a step graphically described as 'shoving dog shit down people's throats' by a retired, dissident professor at the Chinese Communist Party Central School, Cai Xia. Ms Cai took the precaution of emigrating to America in 2019 before coming out in June 2020 with harsh criticisms of Xi's regime, describing him as 'a mafia boss' and stating in an interview with American media that 'China's communist party does not have the strength or the ability to take the country forward'. In August 2020 she was expelled from the Chinese Communist Party, and had her retirement benefits taken away, as a lesson to other potential party insider dissidents.

The ending of the presidential term limit was also directly criticised by a law professor at the leading Tsinghua University. Xu Zhangrun, who had become a thorn in the government's side, told friends that his article criticising the government's handling of the coronavirus outbreak would probably be his last. Sure enough, early in the morning of 6 July 2020, about twenty people appeared at his apartment in Beijing to take him away, together with his computer and all his papers. At the time of this writing, he has not been seen since his arrest.

Another important dissident who emerged during the early months of 2020 was Fang Fang, a well-known Chinese writer and long-time Wuhan resident, who started keeping a diary at the beginning of the 60-day COVID lockdown of Wuhan, where the virus is thought to have started. Using a pseudonym close to her real name, Fang used her daily diary to criticise the government, both in Wuhan and in Beijing, for its mendacity and incompetence. After writing the diary every evening, she posted it online on Chinese social media — Weibo, the Chinese equivalent of Twitter — where for several hours, in the middle of the night, it could be read by, commented on and re-transmitted between millions of Chinese online readers, before being removed several hours later by China's internet censors. It is estimated that about four million people read the Wuhan Diary of Fang Fang every day, and many more have read it since late March when Fang Fang stopped writing it, especially as the diary has been published in English. The diary drew attention because it records everyday details from her life in Wuhan, like the weather and what she ate for breakfast, along with comments on the development of COVID and on the handling of the virus by the local officials, many of which are critical in a way which all Chinese people could understand. This style gives her a very believable voice, of compassion, intelligence, and concern for her fellow man and woman, together with criticism of Chinese officialdom — meaning, of course, the party. She refers to the reliance of local officials in Wuhan on clear guidelines set by the central government in Beijing, otherwise they won't act, for fear of doing something wrong. She laughs at the party's efforts to create a triumphant virus story celebrating China's resilience, with the party at its core, and with Xi at the head of the party. That's the system which Xi Jinping has established, based on fear, punishment and reality distortion, which allowed the virus to get out of control in January in Wuhan because local officials suppressed the reporting system set up after the 2003 SARS epidemic in China. Appropriate action was not taken until long after the virus had taken firm hold in China, and had spread far and wide beyond China.

The news that these Chinese internet commentators have been recruited by the government in their tens and hundreds to suppress Fang Fang's diary reports is consistent with China's growing success in controlling all forms of media in China, including the internet. Twenty years ago, most people believed that the then new internet would bring liberalism to China because it could not be controlled, and through it, Chinese people everywhere would be able to interact with, exchange ideas with and learn from the rest of the world. But China has enough educated young people, and the electronic and algorithmic tools, to enable its government to penetrate and control all forms of free expression online. President Xi's increasingly oppressive dictatorship uses a variety of tools to identify, watch and manipulate the Chinese population.

Ironically, this kind of control is very useful when it comes to taking the strong measures needed to control the COVID-19 virus. Both the spread of the virus from Wuhan around the world, and China's success in controlling the virus within its own borders are attributable to the system of fear and control which President Xi has put in place.

The spread from Wuhan was caused by the fear of local officials to report bad news, and to act without orders from Beijing; the lockdowns and strict control measures put in place in China since January, which were effective for a time in containing the spread of the virus, were only possible in a highly authoritarian system.

In my opinion, the origin of this new Chinese dictatorship led by Xi is to be found in the perceived vulnerability of the ruling Chinese Communist Party. When Chinese social media really took off around 2010, with the advent of smartphones and faster internet speeds, the party discovered, by listening in on the conversations of ordinary people, what Chinese people thought about them: corrupt, incompetent, and interested more in furthering their own and their family's interests than in ruling the country progressively and fairly. The scandal in 2012 involving a possible future Chinese leader, Bo Xilai, and his wife was a disaster for the party, because a foreigner — an Englishman, Neil Heywood — was involved. The details of his murder by Bo's wife Gu Kailai, and the subsequent helicopter escape to Beijing of Bo's police chief, Wang Lijun, from certain liquidation by Chongqing Communist Party boss Bo, which normally would have been hushed up by the party, were spread all over the Western media. The news quickly crossed the Great Chinese Wall of censorship to become public knowledge inside China as well.

Two things followed from this very public event. Xi Jinping, not Bo Xilai, became China's president. And with its survival at stake, the party decided that it had to clamp down on the Westernisation of Chinese culture and education. The party's primacy had to be restored. Glorification of the country's achievements provided a background to the party's elevation and to the pre-eminence of President Xi. Since 2015, the story has been one of increasing concentration of power by President Xi, combined with the recruitment of every part of Chinese society, including the organs of the economy as well as security, to support him and the party.

The opposition within China to these developments is clear and non-trivial. But the government has reacted swiftly and powerfully to every threat from within. A well-known opponent of President Xi, Ren Zhiqiang, a party member and real-estate tycoon (known in China as 'The Cannon') who recently described the president as 'a clown', in 2020 was arrested and sentenced to eighteen years in prison for various offences related to the long-running anti-corruption campaign. Most people thought that when the new president started an anti-corruption campaign shortly after taking office, that he was just following his predecessors who had paid lip-service to party corruption by instituting similar campaigns, only for them to fizzle out after a few months. But Xi's anti-corruption campaign has proved an important tool for him to gain public support, while neutralising his opponents. The campaign shows no signs of stopping, and is one important part of the range of tools used by the president to maintain and strengthen his position.

One key question in the next decade for China, and the world, is whether the dissidents (for whom a considerable number of party members have sympathy) can ever succeed in gaining enough support within China to force President Xi to step down. Xi has fought a long battle with the other main faction within the party which was led by former President Jiang Zemin, but Jiang is dead, and his former powerbase has been weakened by Xi's anti-corruption drive. The impetus to remove Xi is unlikely to come from that source, although it would provide important support to an anti-Xi initiative which came from somewhere else.

The key to Xi's position is his support within the military and the security services. But Xi's top-to-bottom restructuring of the Chinese military in 2015-16, which was accompanied by some high level arrests of senior generals who were found to have been selling senior military positions for cash, has given him control over the single most important powerbroker in China. Meanwhile, his external aggression, especially towards Taiwan, and talk of war with America, rallies Chinese patriotic support behind Xi. In short, although there is considerable opposition within the party to his increasingly dictatorial rule, it's hard to see how Xi can be toppled.

My expectation is that Xi Jinping will continue to be the President of China for at least another decade. If so, then the future trend in China over the medium term at least will consist of ever tighter control in domestic matters, further advances in the future weapons of computerised data collection and analysis, and continued assertiveness outside China, with pressure on Taiwan as the near-term focus of Chinese aggression. Xi has made the recovery of Taiwan the centrepiece of his Asian policy. With America committed by law to defend Taiwanese independence (Taiwan Relations Act 1 January 1979), the stage is set for a superpower showdown in the Taiwan Straits. This stand-off has existed since the Communists took over China in 1949, at which time America threw in its lot with the Republicans under Chiang Kai-Shek. But China's new military capability and increasing dominance of the South China Sea has made a Chinese victory in the Taiwan Straits possible, for the first time since 1949. As the cost of defending Taiwan grows and the likelihood of success diminishes, America may decide that this game is no longer worth the candle. In this case, wiggle room which the drafting of the Taiwan Relations Act permits, will be fully utilised. That outcome is quite likely. Mainland Chinese control of Taiwan would mark decisively the shift of power from America to China, and not just in east Asia.

Other probable consequences of an extended period of rule by Xi Jinping include the continuation and extension of the Belt-and-Road project which connects China to central Asia, Europe and East Africa largely by land routes, and steady growth in China's military and naval capabilities which will make the possibility of a successful American intervention in east Asia increasingly difficult and improbable.

Many economists and strategists have argued that the main threat to a scenario of growing Chinese power will come from some kind of sustained weakness in China's economy. The first reason to think this expectation may be wrong is to look at the success of economic and market commentators on China over the last twenty years. The balance of well-informed expectation has always been in favour of a Chinese economic collapse, led by over-indebtedness, and underpinned by the economic inefficiency of China's state-owned sector which controls the country's main economic arteries. Yet, in 2008, it was America, not China that looked like collapsing. An American think-tank, the Rhodium Group, estimates that China has produced 40% of global economic growth since the 2008 financial crisis. Over the five years 2015-19, according to IMF statistics, China's economy grew by 38%, and America's by 13%. And for the COVID-19 years of 2020 and 2021, China's economy is projected (at this time of writing, in later 2020) to grow by 10%, and the United States to shrink by 3%. By the end of 2021, China's economy (measured by the IMF in purchasing power terms), would total $31 trillion, 40% larger than America's. These measures, admittedly mostly backward-looking, do not support the idea of a Chinese economic collapse, and they do demonstrate that most expectations of China's economic development have been plain wrong, at least so far.

But Xi Jinping's commitments to market-oriented economic reform, made in November 2013, have not been implemented. Instead of market based reforms, ever greater control has been extended into the economic sphere, via an extension of party power and surveillance into every Chinese economic entity, and by the subordination of successful private enterprises, some very large, to the party's dictate and control. The message that everything and everyone in China serves the state, and therefore the party, has been spread far and wide. Is this phenomenon of Chinese 'state capitalism'. sustainable? Or will it collapse under the weight of its own inertia and indebtedness?

Conventional modern economic theory holds that a state-directed economy will allocate resources badly, leading to economic waste, inefficiency, supply bottlenecks, unsatisfied demand, and a greater likelihood of economic and financial crisis. But in China, this simple analysis is undermined by the fact that 50-60% of economic output in the country comes not from government controlled companies, but from the private sector. Although state owned and state run companies, some of them huge, control the vital sinews of the Chinese economy, including banking and financial services, power and water utilities, telecoms, air travel and so on, they do not dominate the economy in terms of economic activity or employment overall. Much of China's private sector is world-class in productivity and efficiency. For example, in 2019, China, competing with famous foreign brands like VW, BMW and Audi, produced 21.4 million passenger cars to meet its own demand, amounting to 37% of global car output (source: Statista). At such a scale, it obviously makes commercial sense to localise production of inputs in China, including auto components, and where possible, raw materials. As a consequence, virtually all the local suppliers to the Chinese car manufacturers are privately owned Chinese companies, many of them formed as joint ventures with foreign parts suppliers from Germany, Japan, America and so on. The same dominance of private ownership is repeated across many other Chinese sectors, especially those which are dedicated to export overseas, or where large amounts of start-up capital are not required. It's true that in recent years, these private Chinese companies have been brought within the party's control. But they retain the dynamism and efficiency which made them viable and surviving economic entities, because if they fail, they know they won't be bailed out by the government (although they might be acquired by a competitor).

It is not accurate to describe the Chinese economy as dependent on government direction and support, and bloated with excess employment. Much of it is efficient and productive. That's the main reason why China's economy remains so resilient to shocks.

The Chinese financial sector has been identified as another potential source of weakness. Bank assets have grown by four times in China since 2008, and the Chinese banking system is now the world's largest, equivalent in 2020 to 40% of global GDP. Such a credit expansion has never been seen before, at least in modern world history, and there is a fear that it could be inherently unstable and unmanageable. Yet, major financial shocks were experienced in 2013, 2015 and in 2018 in China, for various different reasons, but the Chinese regulators and the system as a whole proved flexible and sure-footed enough to avert a crisis. Currently, it is thought by some observers that the gradual withdrawal of Beijing's support from troubled Chinese financial institutions could be the source of a major crisis. But another interpretation of this withdrawal of explicit government support is that it encourages market participants to pay more attention to balance sheets and other financial measures, and therefore paves the way for a better pricing of risk. This would reduce, not increase, the likelihood of a major financial crisis in China.

The fact is that the Chinese Government has been able to manage China's remarkable expansion very successfully so far, and in so doing, has confounded the expectations of many Western commentators. But China is not risk-free. The main economic risk, in my opinion, is political: the rejection of Xi and his system of government, which could undermine, at least for a time, the internal and external credibility of the Beijing Government and its huge apparatus to intervene in and successfully manage the economy. A sudden, violent change in China's politics would certainly have huge economic and geopolitical effects which could easily get out of control. This fear is shared by many Chinese, and is a major reason why many relatively free-thinking, and 'liberal' people in China continue to tolerate the status quo. The cost of sudden change in China could be extremely high, and many prefer to wait, instead, although the wait may be a long one.

In the long run, however, as the number of wealthy, well-travelled people in China grows, I expect China's governance to evolve toward a more pluralistic and less dictatorial system, probably by way of changes within the party as a first step. But the system that emerges will owe much more to Chinese ideas than to Western ones, and it won't happen soon. In all probability, we face a one-party Chinese system that attempts to become more acceptable to the rest of the world by demonstrating its ability to manage China's ascent competently and peacefully, We shouldn't expect China to fail just because their system s different to our own.